The
Home and Country
Cookbook

Rosemary Wadey

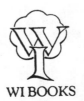

WI BOOKS

This selection of recipes first published 1991 by W.I. Books Ltd,
in association with Southgate Publishers Ltd.
Glebe House, Church Street, Crediton, Devon EX17 2AF.

Printed and bound in Great Britain by Devonshire Press, Torquay

British Library Cataloguing in Publication Data.
A CIP catalogue record for this book is available from the British Library.

ISBN 0 947990 75 5

Front cover: Pasta Beanpot; Cartwheel Salad; Noodles with Ham and Raisins.
Back cover: Danish Pastries; Savarin.

Contents

Introduction   7

Soups and Starters   12
Home-made Stocks   13
Tomato and Courgette Soup   14
Potato and Tarragon Soup   14
Smoked Haddock Soup   15
Cream of Artichoke Soup   16
Mixed Vegetable Broth   17
Cock–a–Leekie Soup   17
Moules Marinière   18
Mackerel Puffs with Horseradish Dip   19
Fish Terrine with Smoked Salmon   20
Duck Terrine   21
Cheese and Walnut Pâté   21
Chicken Liver Pâté   22
Avocado and Melon with Raspberry Vinaigrette   22
Marinated Mushrooms   23
Spinach Roulade   24

Light Meals, Snacks and Pasta   25
Shortcrust Pastry   26
Poacher's Roll   26
Blue Cheese Quiche   27
Baked Mushrooms   28
Hot Cheese Soufflé and Variations   28
Cheese and Bacon Granary Bars   29
Potted Meat   30
Savoury Gougère   30
Chinese Egg Rolls   31
Sausage Tattie 'Ash   32
Pasta Beanpot   33
Cartwheel Salad   34
Noodles with Ham and Raisins   34
Bacon and Bean Lasagne   35
Vegetable Pasta Bake   36

Vegetables and Salads   37
Potato Galette with Chives   38
Mushroom and Sesame Stir Fry   38
Boston Baked Beans   39
Nut Burgers   42
Leek and Onion Tartlets   42
Spinach and Walnut Pancakes   43

French Dressing 44
Mayonnaise 44
Cooked Salad Dressing 45
Special Potato Salad 46
Avocado and Egg Salad 46
Rosy Red Chicken Salad 47
Leek, Bacon and Pineapple Salad 47

Fish 48
Cider Soused Herrings 49
Old Fashioned Kedgeree 49
Cod à la Grecque 50
Mackerel Rolls with Orange Cider Sauce 51
Haddock Pulao 52
Goujons of Plaice 52
Seafish Pie 53
Trout with Watercress and Lemon Stuffing 54
Sweet and Sour Halibut Steaks 55
Special Fish Pie 55
Crab au Gratin 56
Salmon Mousse 57
Salmon en Croûte 58

Meat and Poultry 59
Beef: Spicy Brisket Pot Roast 61
Devilled Meatballs 62
Mairangi Beef 63
Perryland Steak 63
Barlavington Hotpot 64

Lamb: Lamb Quickie Grills 65
Roast Lamb with Cashew Nut Stuffing 65
Apricot Lamb en Croûte 66
Lamb Steaks Wairapa 67

Pork and Ham: Somerset Pork 67
Catalina Pork 68
Pork Satay with Yellow Rice 69
Honey Baked Ham 69

Chicken: Polynesian Chicken 70
Marinated Chicken with Mustard 71
Red Chicken Curry 71
Chicken en Cocotte 72
Normandy Chicken 72

Turkey: Turkey Boulangère 73
Turkey Escalopes Stilton 74
Turkey Carbonnade 75

Others: Oxtail Casserole 75
Roast Duck with Spiced Pears 76
Pheasant with Walnuts and Cranberries 77
Game Pie 78
Venison Casserole 79
Rabbit Casserole 80

Puddings and Desserts 81
Apple and Pear Pudding 82
Hot Fruit Soufflé 82
Christmas Pudding 83
Coffee Walnut Crêpes 84
Bread, Butter and Apple Pudding 85
Crêpes Suzette 86
Orange and Lemon Pudding 86
Apple Strudel 87
Old Fashioned Treacle Tart 88
Coffee Syllabubs 89
Coffee Walnut Meringues 89
Coffee Malakoff Cake 90
Strawberry and Orange Boodle 91
Yogurt Mousse with Strawberries and Redcurrant Sauce 91
Gooseberry Ice Cream 92
Brown Bread Ice Cream 93
Ice Cream Bombe 93
Chocolate Soufflé 94
Burnt Cream 95
Hazelnut and Peach Cheesecake 95
Paris Brest de Pommes 96
Chocolate Chestnut Gâteau 97

Teatime 99
Hazelnut or Almond Tuiles 100
Honey Cinnamon Buns 100
Brandy Snaps 101
Fruited Flapjacks 101
Scones 102
Welsh Cakes 102
Pinwheel Sandwiches 103
Courgette and Tarragon Quiches 104
Sausage and Salami Rolls 105
Hazelnut Florentines 105
Orange and Cardamom Biscuits 106
Lime Creams 106
Danish Pastries 107
Chocolate Brownies 108
Blueberry and Apple Strudels 109
Ginger Meringues 110

Spiced Whisky Cake   110
Christmas Cake   111
Apple and Spice Cake   112
Cranberry Teabread   112
Victoria Sandwich   113
Bara Brith   114
Gingerbread   115

Party Foods   116
Avocado and Crab Cocktails   117
Soused Pink Trout Fillets   117
Duck with Orange and Cranberry Sauce   118
Brown Rice and Peanut Salad   118
Red Cabbage and Leek Medley   119
Mixed Salad with Fennel and Watercress   119
Chocolate Blackcurrant Gâteau   119
Peach and Banana Syllabubs   120
Pissaladière   121
Salmagundy   122
Rare Beef Rolls with Mustard Mayonnaise   123
Stuffed Pasta Shells   123
Stuffed Tomatoes   124
Nectarine Salad   124
Ruby Wine Cup   125
Ginger Special   125
Rosy Wine Cup   126
Barbary Ale   126
Chairman's Special   126
Sangria   127
Orange Cooler   127

Introduction

Cooking is an essential part of life; everyone has to eat to live and on the whole we enjoy doing so because of the wide range of foods available to us and the almost unlimited ways of preparing, cooking and serving them.

The art of cooking is age old and in many cases is a skill which has been passed down from generation to generation. Only in recent years has it become an important and popular part of the school curriculum, thus beginning to equip both boys and girls away from home with essential skills. However, many of the best cooks today are self taught and have picked up their knowledge from watching and asking others and following cookery books; though there are those, too, who have been highly trained and, as professionals, can produce anything asked for.

To my mind, once the necessary basic skills have been mastered, you can then progress rapidly on to the more exciting and complicated cookery but it is not always these complicated recipes that turn out to be the best. Good, basic cooking takes a lot of beating and reasonably simple dishes can be transformed into masterpieces by the odd addition thought up by the cook, and by presenting and garnishing them to perfection. So many good dishes are spoilt by poor presentation, perhaps through lack of time but more often because the cook doesn't bother – and good presentation is vital. Another important factor is to serve hot food really hot on warmed plates, not lukewarm on cold plates; and if the dish is meant to be cold then so it should be, having been chilled sufficiently according to the recipe.

The recipes in this book have been selected to cover all tastes and circumstances. There are economy dishes and exotic ones; some very quick and easy, others taking much longer to prepare and a little more thought and skill; some meatless, others low calorie; but it should be possible to produce all of them successfully, even for the beginner, provided the recipes are followed correctly. Ingredients are listed in the order in which they are used. The oven temperature is picked out; it is easy to see what temperature is required and to remember to turn the oven on before starting, because some of the recipes will fail if kept waiting while the oven heats up. Preparation of the ingredients is mainly mentioned in the ingredients list; other processes are in the method; and at the end of each ingredients list there is a rough guide to preparation and cooking times.

It is very important when following these recipes to use either the metric or the imperial measures. They should not be mixed because in some cases they are not exact conversions and this will affect the result of the finished dish. Oven temperatures are given first in centigrade, then fahrenheit and then the gas equivalent. Those with fan ovens can place food anywhere in the oven; conventional ovens tend to be slightly hotter at the top and a little cooler towards the bottom so food should be placed accordingly. Some of the very modern ovens are supposed to be 'faster cooking' and in these cases it is wise to consult the instruction book which will tell you how to adapt either the cooking temperature or times accordingly.

With the wide range of fresh food available today all the recipes in this book can be made using fresh ingredients. However, many foods are frozen extremely successfully and consequently are available throughout the year rather than just keeping to their normal seasons. Many people like to freeze their own foods, too, particularly when there are gluts of vegetables or fruit in the garden, or there is an opportunity to freeze down meat, poultry, fish or game when it is bought in bulk. It is wise to use frozen foods as and when necessary but please take care to use them properly. All vegetables and fruit can be used from frozen unless otherwise stated in the recipes but with meat, poultry and fish I advise thorough thawing before cooking and for none of the recipes in this book do I advise cooking from frozen. Once thawed the food will deteriorate more quickly than in its fresh state, so always cook as soon as possible. Many cooked dishes freeze well, too, and those suitable for freezing are indicated in the individual recipes.

The selection of recipes in this book should provide ideas for all occasions. All the recipes should be easy to follow and include some old favourites, some regional specialities and hopefully many new ideas to tempt and encourage you to try them.

Hints and tips

List of terms and methods

To baste – to spoon or pour hot melted fat or dripping or sometimes other liquid over meat, poultry, vegetables etc., to keep it moist during baking or roasting. Use a spoon or special meat basting 'bulb'.

To blanch – to put prepared vegetables or sometimes fruit into a pan of boiling water, allow to come back to boil, then boil for the suggested time which is always short, such as ½ to 3 minutes. Drain, plunge immediately into cold running water and, when cold, drain again very thoroughly. Used prior to freezing and also to take the 'edge' off raw vegetables or to tone down extra strong vegetables such as peppers, leeks etc.

To emulsify – when making mayonnaise and other egg–based sauces the process of mixing eggs with oil by beating hard and adding the oil drop by drop is called emulsifying, as when whisking oil and other ingredients together for a dressing.

To glaze – to brush pastry or other items with beaten egg, milk or egg white before cooking to give a golden and shiny appearance when cooked; also to cover fruit in a flan etc., with a melted jam or arrowroot glaze.

To pare – to cut off something very thinly, e.g. the rind from a lemon, lime or orange (free of white pith), green skin off a cucumber etc. A potato peeler is ideal for this task, although you can also use a small vegetable knife or one of the other gadgets available for specific purposes.

To purée – to make something completely smooth which has been cooked and is either full of lumpy ingredients (e.g. soup) or is just unintentionally lumpy. Either rub through a sieve, with the help of a wooden spoon, or put into a food processor or blender and switch on until smooth. A mouli–blender can also be used.

To shred – to cut something such as cabbage, vegetables, marmalade oranges, etc., into very thin slices or strands. It can be done by hand, on a large electric mixer with the appropriate attachment or in a food processor using one of the shredding plates.

To cut into julienne strips – first pare the rind or skin off thinly using a potato peeler and then cut these pieces into very narrow strips of appropriate length. Citrus rinds, carrots etc., then need to be cooked in boiling water for about 5 minutes and cooled and drained before use.

To skin a tomato – dip the tomato into a pan of boiling water for about 30 seconds. Remove immediately and put into a bowl of cold water. Using a sharp, small knife make a nick in the skin and it should then simply peel off.

To slake – to blend arrowroot or cornflour with the minimum of cold water before it is added to a sauce. Once dissolved, a little of the sauce should be added to the slaked mixture, then it all should be returned to the pan and brought to the boil, stirring continuously until thickened.

To whip – to whip cream or eggs with a hard whisk or fork, using a light circular stroke.

To whisk – a faster way of beating a batter or whipping cream or egg whites until just frothy or really stiff, using a rotary whisk, hand–held electric mixer or large free–standing electric mixer. A flat or balloon whisk can also be used, provided you have a strong arm!

To measure liquid – use a jug with the measurements on the side. Metric measurements are in millilitres and litres; imperial measurements in pints and fluid ounces; and American measurements in cups. Remember an American cup is 8 fl oz/250 ml, whilst an imperial cup is 10 fl oz/½ pint/300 mls.

To measure a level spoonful – use a set of measuring spoons for ease. They are available in sizes of 1 tablespoon; 1 teaspoon; ½ teaspoon and ¼ teaspoon. Fill with the dry ingredient and use a knife to level off the top to be absolutely accurate. Liquid measures are also available. Sets of cup measures are also available.

To measure syrup or honey – warm the jug or spoon then brush lightly all over with oil. The measured syrup will then slowly slide off the spoon or pour out of the jug without sticking. For larger amounts, particularly if the syrup is to be warmed, put the saucepan on the scales, note the weight and then add the appropriate amount of syrup.

Oven temperature guide

	Electricity		Gas Mark
	°C	°F	
Very cool	110	225	¼
	120	250	½
Cool	140	275	1
	150	300	2
Moderate	160	325	3
	180	350	4
Moderately Hot	190	375	5
Fairly Hot	200	400	6
Hot	220	425	7
Very Hot	230	450	8
	240	475	9

Safe Storage of Food

Bacteria are everywhere and many foods rely on certain types of bacteria for their production, but these are of course completely harmless. There are only a few types of bacteria which cause illness, but it makes sense to take as much care as possible to prevent any possibilities of harmful bacteria growing on food.

To ensure the highest possible standards there are many checks along the way until the food reaches the consumer – then it is up to you.

Take care when buying all foods that they look fresh and clean, that the premises where you buy look clean, and the staff likewise. Check the dates on goods to ensure they are still current. Don't buy damaged packs. Don't buy from frozen food cabinets that look overfilled, which might possibly cut down the storage temperature of some of the foods.

Once home, pack fresh foods separately and make sure fresh meat is wrapped and cannot contaminate other foods. Put frozen foods immediately into the freezer; if possible, take an insulated container if you know you may be delayed on the way back to the freezer, to prevent foods beginning to thaw.

Make sure your refrigerator is clean and that it is cold enough. Refrigerators cannot kill bacteria but do slow down the growth of most common bugs. It should be below 5°C/41°F.

Freezers

These should be kept at –18°C/0°F, which stops bacteria multiplying but does not kill them. Note the storage or freezing instructions when stocking your freezer and try to defrost the freezer when stocks are low. This temperature is found on a 3–star freezer, but some which are 4–star reach even lower. If you want to freeze your own food, you must have a freezer with a 'quick–freeze' section which ensures rapid freezing before storage. This usually means a switch put on several hours before required and then switched back again to normal after 12–24 hours. It is advisable with fresh foods, to freeze only 10 per cent of the capacity of the freezer in any 24 hours; ready–frozen foods can be added as required.

Frozen Food Compartment of the Refrigerator

There is a star rating given by refrigerator and frozen food manufacturers which is a useful guide as to how long you can keep frozen foods in the frozen food compartment of a domestic refrigerator or in the freezer section of a fridge/freezer. There is a star symbol * to denote the storage temperature.

Maximum temperature of frozen food compartment	Maximum storage time	
	Frozen Foods	Ice cream
* –6°C/21°F	up to 1 week	1 day
** –12°C/10°F	up to 1 month	up to 2 weeks
*** –18°C/0°F	up to 3 months	up to 3 months

Eggs

The Government has lifted restrictions on using raw eggs in cooking. However, there are one or two points that are worth noting. It may be wise to avoid serving dishes containing uncooked eggs to the elderly, sick people, toddlers and babies and possibly pregnant women. This does not mean there is anything wrong at all, but people in these categories are more susceptible to infection than others. It may be better to serve them properly cooked with the white solid and the yolk solid or almost solid. If the eggs are pasteurized there is no problem for anyone.

Points of Interest

All spoon measures in this book are level unless otherwise stated.

Eggs used are size 2 or 3 unless otherwise stated.
3 level teaspoons equal 1 level tablespoon.
8 tablespoons liquid equals 5 fl oz/4 pt/150ml.

When using a pressure cooker always consult the manufacturer's instructions before commencing.

Cooking with microwaves has become very popular. There are now many cookery books published solely for the use of microwave owners and these, together with the manufacturer's handbooks, do need to be well read if you are a new user. Also check the wattage of your particular machine because most recipes are based on using a 650 watt model, but if yours is different the cooking times need to be adapted slightly, and this will be explained.

SOUPS AND STARTERS

INTRODUCTION

The best soups have a base of home-made stock made from raw or cooked bones flavoured with vegetables; or, for vegetarians a strong vegetable stock made with a wide variety of root and green vegetables with the essential addition of a bouquet garni. Bone stocks need long slow cooking for about 3–4 hours; vegetable stocks take about an hour whilst fish stock requires only 30–40 minutes. A pressure cooker speeds up the process but always follow the manufacturer's instructions for the best results. If time defeats you, then use one of the excellent varieties of stock cubes available, but be careful as they tend to be on the salty side.

Many soups freeze well but remember to allow a headspace in the container as liquids expand as they freeze. Stock will also freeze for about 1–2 months but it is a good idea to boil it down to half quantity and freeze it in concentrated form to save valuable freezer space and then add an equal amount of water when it is used. It is best to add cream, eggs, extra milk and all garnishes to soup when it has been thawed and reheated. Remember, too, that it is essential to reheat thawed soup gently until it boils and then simmer for a few minutes before serving. Stock or soup can be stored for 1–2 days in the refrigerator but it should then be boiled up and cooled again before further storage.

When it comes to starters the selection of recipes is unlimited and includes hot and cold; fish, meat and seafood; vegetables and salads; soufflés and roulades; pâtés and terrines. The most important factor is to choose a starter which blends appropriately with the rest of the meal and for the busy cook it is often a good idea to select something that can be prepared or made earlier in the day or even the day before; so planning a well–balanced menu not only pleases your guests but also helps the work–load of the cook.

A starter should look attractive and appetizing and never be so large or heavy that it spoils the rest of the meal – it should, in fact, be an 'appetizer'. Take care to balance cream, pastry and rich foods with lighter salad or fruit starters and choose a 'dry' starter such as pâté if you are following it with a casserole; try a blander starter with a spicy main course; and offer a hot one before a cold main course. Remember that soups and many starters also make excellent light lunches or snack meals and need not be solely restricted to the first course of a meal.

STOCKS

The secret of a good soup lies in the basic stock used and here are the relevant recipes to make the best possible soups.

Preparation time: *20 minutes*
Cooking time: *2–4 hours*

White Stock

Put 900 g (2 lb) veal or veal and lamb bones into a saucepan with 2.2 litres (4 pints) water, a squeeze of lemon juice, 2 sliced onions, 2–3 sliced carrots and a bouquet garni. Bring to the boil, remove any scum and cover. Simmer for about 4 hours. Strain, cool and when cold remove any fat from the surface.

Brown Stock

Brown 450 g (1 lb) each of marrow bones and cut-up shin of beef in a hot oven (220°C/425°F/Gas Mark 6) for 30–60 minutes, then put into a saucepan with 2.2 litres (4 pints) water, 2 sliced onions, 2 sliced carrots, 2 sliced sticks of celery and a bouquet garni. Continue as for white stock.

Poultry or Game Stock

Put the carcass of a chicken, turkey or game bird (raw or cooked) into a saucepan, breaking it up as necessary. Add the giblets if available and 2 sliced onions, 2 sliced carrots, 2 sticks of celery and a bouquet garni or bay leaf. Cover with water and continue as for white stock, but simmer for only 2–3 hours, and give an occasional good stir.

Vegetable Stock

Put 2 sliced onions and 450–675 g (1–1½ lb) mixed, roughly chopped vegetables (e.g. carrots, turnips, swede, leeks, celery etc.) into a pan with a bouquet garni and 1–1.4 litres (2–3 pints) water. Bring to the boil, cover and simmer for an hour. Strain and use.

Fish Stock

Put the fish bones, skin and trimmings or a cod or salmon head into a pan with ½ lemon, 1 sliced onion, 2 sliced carrots, a bouquet garni, a few sprigs of parsley and 10 black peppercorns. Cover with cold water, bring to the boil and simmer for 40 minutes. Strain and use.

Tomato and Courgette Soup

A delicious soup, especially good to make when there is a glut of tomatoes and courgettes. Frozen tomatoes can be used for this recipe.

Serves 6

40 g (1½oz) butter or margarine
1 large onion, peeled and chopped
l large carrot, peeled and chopped
1–2 sticks celery, chopped
2 level tablespoons flour
1.1 litres (2 pints) stock (chicken, beef
   or vegetable)
2 level tablespoons of tomato purée

450 g (1 lb) tomatoes, peeled and
   chopped
salt and pepper
1 bay leaf
2 large courgettes, trimmed and
   coarsely grated
1 tablespoon wine vinegar
pinch of sugar

Preparation time: 20 minutes
Cooking time: 45 minutes

Melt the fat in a pan and add the onion, carrot and celery. Fry gently until soft but not coloured, stirring frequently. Add the flour, cook for a minute or so and then gradually stir in the stock and bring to the boil. Stir in the tomato purée, tomatoes, seasonings and bay leaf and simmer, covered, for about 20 minutes or until very soft; discard the bay leaf. Cool the soup a little then purée in a blender or food processor. Return to a clean pan with the courgettes and vinegar and bring back to the boil. Simmer for 5 minutes, uncovered, then adjust the seasonings, adding sugar to taste. Serve with croûtons (see below) which can be made 24 hours in advance and stored in an airtight container.

Freezing recommended: for up to 2 months

Croûtons – Remove the crusts from 3 slices of bread and cut into dice. Heat 50 g (2 oz) butter with garlic and herbs (or plain butter) in a frying pan and fry the cubes of bread gently in it, turning frequently until a pale golden brown. Drain on absorbent kitchen paper before serving.

Potato and Tarragon Soup

A good warming winter soup, but equally good when served chilled in the summer when it needs a little extra milk or single cream to achieve the required consistency.

Serves 4–6

40 g (1½ oz) butter or margarine
1 large or 2 smaller onions, peeled and
   chopped

l clove garlic, crushed
600 ml (l pint) vegetable stock
450 g (1 lb) potatoes, peeled and diced

salt and pepper
3 level tablespoons freshly chopped
   tarragon
   or 1½ level tablespoons dried tarragon

45 ml (¾ pint) milk, approx
2 carrots, peeled and coarsely grated

Preparation time: 20 minutes
Cooking time: 30 minutes

Melt the fat in a saucepan and fry the onions and garlic gently until soft, but not coloured, stirring frequently. Add the stock, potatoes, seasonings and 2 tablespoons fresh or 1 tablespoon dried tarragon and bring to the boil. Cover and simmer gently until very tender, about 25–30 minutes. Cool the soup a little then purée in a blender or food processor and return to a clean pan. Add the milk, carrots and remaining tarragon and bring back to the boil. Simmer gently for 5 minutes then adjust the seasonings and consistency, adding a little more milk or stock if too thick. Serve with croûtons or garlic bread (see below).

Freezing recommended: for up to 2 months

Garlic bread – Take a short French or Vienna loaf and cut into slices about 2.5 cm (1 inch) wide but leaving a hinge on the base. Mash about 75 g (3 oz) butter with 2–4 crushed cloves of garlic and use to spread on each slice of bread. Reassemble the loaf and wrap in foil then put into a fairly hot oven (200°C/400°F/Gas Mark 6) for 15–20 minutes. Serve hot.

Smoked Haddock Soup

A good fishy soup which can have the consistency altered to your own particular fancy and the occasion. Take care adding salt for the fish itself can be salty.

Serves 5–6

225 g (½ lb) smoked haddock
1 onion, peeled and finely chopped
600 ml (1 pint) water
600 ml (1 pint) milk
salt and pepper

225–350 g (8–12 oz) hot mashed potato
25 g (1 oz) butter
grated rind of ¼ lemon
1 tablespoon lemon juice
2 tablespoons freshly chopped parsley

Preparation time: 20 minutes
Cooking time: 40 minutes

Put the fish into a saucepan with the onion and water. Cover and simmer gently until tender, about 15 minutes. Remove the fish from the liquor and remove the skin and bones. Flake the fish finely and keep aside and return the skin and bones to the cooking liquor. Simmer for 10 minutes then strain this liquid into a clean saucepan. Add the flaked fish, milk and seasonings (taking care with the salt) and bring back to the boil. Simmer for 3 minutes and then gradually whisk in sufficient mashed potato to give the required consistency. Stir in the butter, lemon rind and juice and parsley and simmer for 1–2 minutes. Serve very hot with hot crusty bread or savoury butter toasts (see below).

Freezing recommended: *for up to 6 weeks*

Savory butter toasts – use a packet of savoury butter with lemon and parsley or black pepper and simply pipe or spread onto 12–18 mini French toasts. Alternatively, blend 75 g (3 oz) butter with the grated rind of 1 lemon and 3 tablespoons freshly chopped parsley; or with 1–2 tablespoons coarsely ground pepper suitable for adding to steaks.

Cream of Artichoke Soup

Jerusalem artichokes have a very distinct flavour and make one of the best possible soups. Their disadvantage is their uneven shape which makes them difficult to peel. They can be used unpeeled and well scrubbed but this will produce a pale creamy brown rather than an almost white soup.

Serves 5–6

900 g (2 lb) Jerusalem artichokes
juice of 1 lemon
50 g (2 oz) butter or margarine
2 onions, peeled and chopped
1.2 litres (2 pints) chicken stock
salt and pepper
1 bay leaf

1 blade mace or ¼ level teaspoon
  ground mace
1 tablespoon lemon juice
150 ml (¼ pint) single or double cream
fried croûtons and chopped parsley to
  garnish

Preparation time: *20 minutes*
Cooking time: *45 minutes*

Peel the artichokes and immediately plunge into cold water to which the juice of 1 lemon has been added to prevent them discolouring; or scrub very thoroughly, cutting out any badly bruised parts. Melt the fat in a large saucepan and fry the onions until soft but not coloured. Cut the artichokes into approx 2.5 cm (1 inch) pieces and add to the pan, turning in the fat until well coated. Cook for a minute or so, then gradually add the stock and bring up to the boil. Season and add the bay leaf, mace and lemon juice. Cover and simmer gently for about 30 minutes or until tender. Discard the bay leaf and blade of mace then purée the soup in a blender or food processor. Return to a clean pan, adjust seasonings and stir in the cream. Reheat gently to just below boiling point and serve with fried croûtons and sprinkled with chopped parsley.

Freezing recommended: *for up to 2 months, adding cream when reheated.*

Mixed Vegetable Broth

A delicious true 'green' soup full of leeks, sprouts and beans which can be altered by using the stock made from a chicken carcass along with the chopped pickings of flesh from the bones added at the end.

Serves 5–6

40 g (1 ½ oz) butter or margarine
1 onion, peeled and sliced
2 leeks, trimmed and sliced
225 g (½ lb) sprouts, trimmed and
    quartered
225 g (½ lb) French beans or cut green
    beans

900 ml (1½ pints) vegetable stock
salt and pepper
1 tablespoon lemon juice
2 teaspoons Worcestershire sauce
pinch of ground nutmeg or mace
300 ml (½ pint) milk
150 ml (¼ pint) single cream

Preparation time: 15 minutes
Cooking time: 45 minutes

Melt the fat in a large saucepan and fry the onion gently for 2–3 minutes until soft. Add leeks, sprouts and beans and toss thoroughly in the fat. Gradually add the stock and bring to the boil. Season well, add lemon juice, Worcestershire sauce and nutmeg or mace and cover the pan. Simmer gently for about 25 minutes or until quite tender. Cool a little, then purée the soup in a blender or food processor. Return to a clean pan with the milk, adding a little extra milk or stock if too thick, then adjust the seasonings and bring back to the boil. Serve with cream swirled into each portion.

Freezing recommended: for up to 2 months, adding the cream when reheated.

Cock–a–Leekie Soup

A traditional soup made from a whole chicken or large carcass with chunky pieces of vegetable in it, suitable to satisfy even the largest of appetites.

Serves 6–8

900 g–1.1. kg (2 – 2½ lb) oven ready
    chicken with giblets
or a large chicken carcass with some
    meat left on it
1 lemon, quartered
40 g (1½ oz) butter or margarine
3 leeks, trimmed and thinly sliced
4 carrots, peeled and thinly sliced (see
    note below)

1 clove garlic, crushed
1 onion, peeled and studded with 6
    whole cloves
1 large bouquet garni
1 bay leaf
water or stock
salt and black pepper
16 no–need–to–soak stoned prunes
freshly chopped parsley to garnish

Preparation time: 25 minutes
Cooking time: 1¾–2 hours

Wipe the chicken inside and out and wash the giblets. Put the lemon into the chicken cavity. Melt the fat in a large saucepan and gently fry the leeks, carrots and garlic for about 5 minutes, stirring to prevent sticking and over-browning. Stand the chicken on the vegetables (or break up the carcass roughly and stand on the vegetables) and add the onion, bouquet garni, bay leaf and giblets, if available. Add enough water or stock to barely cover the chicken and bring to the boil. Season, cover the pan and simmer gently for about an hour. Add the prunes and continue simmering for about 30 minutes or until the chicken is very tender.

Remove the chicken and discard the lemon from the cavity, the bouquet garni and bay leaf, giblets and onion. Remove the cloves from the onion and chop the flesh finely; return to the soup. Strip all or part of the meat from the carcass, discarding the skin. Chop roughly and return to the soup. If using a carcass only, remove all the bones, strip off all the best meat, chop and return to the soup. Reheat, adjust the seasonings and serve piping hot, liberally sprinkled with chopped parsley.

Freezing recommended: *for up to 6 weeks*

Note: the slices of carrot may be cut with a fancy cutter to give a pretty effect to the finished soup.

Moules Marinière

When mussels are available this makes a very good soup. Scrub the shells thoroughly before cooking and remove any beards and pieces of seaweed.

Serves 4–6

Approx 1.4 kg (3 lb) mussels
1 large onion or 2 smaller onions, peeled and finely chopped
1–2 cloves garlic, crushed
2 tablespoons oil
300 ml (½ pint) dry white wine
600 ml (1 pint) water
2 carrots, peeled and very finely
chopped (optional)
2 sticks celery, very finely chopped
2 bay leaves
salt and pepper
25 g (1 oz) butter
2 level tablespoons flour
4–6 tablespoons cream (optional)
freshly chopped parsley to garnish

Preparation time: *30 minutes*
Cooking time: *20 minutes*

Wash the mussels very well in several changes of cold water and discard any that are cracked or do not close completely when given a sharp tap. Put the onion, garlic and oil into a large pan and fry gently for 4–5 minutes until soft but not at all coloured. Add the wine, water, vegetables, bay leaves and seasonings and bring to the boil. Add the mussels, cover the pan and cook gently for a few minutes, shaking the pan from time to time, until most of the mussels have opened.

As they open, remove the mussels and break off the empty half shell. Keep them warm. Boil the liquid hard for a few minutes to reduce a little and discard the bay leaves. Blend the butter and flour together to make a *beurre manié* and then whisk it into the soup, a knob at a time. If liked, add a little cream to the soup, adjust the seasonings and return the mussels to the pan. Heat gently for a few minutes. Serve in large soup bowls sprinkled very generously with chopped parsley and accompanied by hot crusty bread. Put a large bowl in the centre of the table for the discarded mussel shells.

Mackerel Puffs with Horseradish Dip

For a cocktail party make the puffs half the size and serve on cocktail sticks.

Serves 4

Mackerel Puffs:
50 g (2 oz) butter or margarine
150 ml (¼ pint) water
65 g (2½ oz) plain flour, sifted
salt and pepper
pinch of cayenne pepper
1 egg (size 2 or 3), beaten
50 g (2 oz) mature Cheddar cheese,
  finely grated
100g (4 oz) smoked mackerel fillets,
skinned and finely flaked

Horseradish Dip:
150 ml (¼ pint) thick mayonnaise
1 teaspoon Worcestershire sauce
grated rind of 1 lemon
2 teaspoons lemon juice
1 level tablespoon creamed horseradish
1 tablespoon freshly chopped parsley

oil for deep frying
lemon and parsley to garnish

Preparation time: *30 minutes*
Cooking time: *20 minutes*

Melt the butter in the water in a pan and bring to the boil. Add the flour all at once and beat well until smooth so the mixture leaves the sides of the pan clean. Remove from the heat, add seasonings and leave to cool a little. Add the beaten egg a little at a time, beating until the mixture is smooth and glossy, then beat in the cheese and mackerel. Combine all the sauce ingredients and place in a small bowl. Heat the oil in a deep pan until a cube of bread browns in about 20 seconds. Drop or pipe teaspoons of fish mixture into the hot fat, five or six at a time, and fry until puffed up and golden brown all over – about 3–4 minutes. Drain well on absorbent kitchen paper and keep warm until the frying is complete. Garnish with lemon wedges and parsley. Serve hot with the cold sauce.

Note: if you prefer not to use mayonnaise containing raw eggs, replace it with soured cream or thick set natural yoghurt but omit the lemon juice.

Variations: prawns, smoked haddock, smoked salmon etc. can be used in place of the smoked mackerel.

Fish Terrine with Smoked Salmon

Smoked salmon and broccoli add colour and flavour to this terrine which is ideal as a starter or part of a cold buffet table.

Serves 10

575 g (1¼ lb) sole or plaice fillets,
*   skinned*
1 tablespoon lemon juice
salt and pepper
pinch of cayenne pepper
2 egg whites
150 ml (¼ pint) double cream or soured
*   cream*

175 g (6 oz) sliced smoked salmon or
*   salmon pieces*
175 g (6 oz) broccoli spears, blanched
*   and chopped*

To garnish:
cucumber slices
frisée or other lettuce
dill or watercress

Preparation time: *45 minutes*
Cooking time: *1 hour*
Heat the oven to 160°C/325°F/Gas Mark 3.

Purée the raw white fish in a blender or a food processor then add the lemon juice, seasonings and egg whites and continue to purée until smooth. Gradually add the cream with the machine still running. Chill the mixture for an hour or so. Roll the slices of smoked salmon into small rolls or, if pieces are used, cut into strips. Line a loaf tin approx 23 x 12.5 x 7.5 cm (9 x 5 x 3 inches.) with non–stick silicone paper, or grease a similar sized terrine. Line the bottom and sides of the tin or terrine with the fish mixture then arrange two–thirds of the smoked salmon rolls or strips in the space in the centre; cover with the chopped broccoli. Add the remaining white fish mixture and smooth the top evenly. Cover with greased greaseproof or non–stick paper and stand the tin or terrine in a roasting tin with water coming halfway up the sides. Cook in a very moderate oven for 50–60 minutes until set.

Remove from the water bath, leave to cool then drain off any excess cooking liquids. Chill thoroughly. *To serve:* remove the terrine carefully from its container and peel off the paper. Garnish with slices of cucumber, frisée, the reserved smoked salmon and sprigs of dill or watercress.

Freezing recommended: *for up to 1 month*

Duck Terrine

Duck flavoured with orange and port makes an excellent terrine. Oven ready duckling are widely available but when you can find a brace of wild duck the flavour will be even better.

Serves 10

1 oven–ready duckling (approx 2 kg/
   4 ½ lb)
225 g (½ lb) belly pork, skinned
225 g (½ lb) pie veal
1 onion, peeled
1–2 cloves garlic, crushed
40 g (1½ oz) butter, melted
salt and pepper
¼ level teaspoon ground coriander

grated rind of 1 orange
4 tablespoons port
approx 4 tablespoons orange juice

To garnish:
orange slices
fresh bay leaves
aspic jelly (optional)

Preparation time: *45 minutes*
Cooking time: *1½–2 hours*
Heat the oven to 160°C/325°F/Gas Mark 3.

Remove the breasts from the duckling, discard the skin and cut the flesh into strips or cubes. Strip off the rest of the meat from the bones and mince finely with the pork, veal and onion. Add the garlic, melted butter, plenty of salt and pepper, ground coriander, orange rind and port and mix well into a greased terrine or casserole dish and cover with the strips or cubes of duck breast, then cover with the rest of the minced mixture. Cover tightly with greased greaseproof paper, then foil, and stand the dish in a roasting tin with water coming halfway up the sides. Cook in a very moderate oven for 1½–2 hours until the juices run clear when pierced with a skewer.

Remove from the water bath, cool and chill. Decorate with orange slices and bay leaves and if liked, add a thin layer of melted aspic jelly. Chill until set and serve spooned from the dish.

Freezing recommended: *for up to 2 months without the garnish or aspic jelly*

Cheese and Walnut Pâté

This is a bit different from the usual type of pâté but very quick to make and well worth a try.

Serves 5–6

2 sticks of celery, very finely chopped
50 g (2 oz) walnut halves, chopped
1 level tablespoon finely chopped onion
   or spring onions
1 level tablespoon snipped chives

salt and pepper
good dash Worcestershire sauce
1 clove garlic, crushed
¼ level tablespoon grated Parmesan
   cheese (preferably fresh)

75 g (3 oz) mature Cheddar cheese,
   finely grated
225 g (8 oz) cottage cheese

50 g (2 oz) butter, melted
celery leaves to garnish

Preparation time: 20 minutes

Put the celery, walnuts, onions, chives, seasonings, Worcestershire sauce, garlic, coriander and Parmesan cheese into a bowl and mix well. Add the other cheeses and mix thoroughly, breaking down the cottage cheese completely. Finally add the melted butter and mix through. Spoon into a large dish or individual pots and chill until firm. Serve with crusty bread or toast, with a salad garnish that includes celery leaves.

Chicken Liver Pâté

An old favourite that is both quick and easy to make.

Serves 6

1 onion, peeled and finely chopped
1–2 cloves garlic, crushed
50 g (2 oz) butter or margarine
450 g (1 lb) chicken livers
2 rashers of bacon, derinded and
   chopped (optional)
salt and pepper

2 tablespoons red wine
good pinch of ground allspice
2 tablespoons double cream

To garnish:
melted butter
capers
fresh bay leaves

Preparation time: 20 minutes
Cooking time: 20 minutes

Fry the onion and garlic very gently in the butter until soft but not coloured. Wash and drain the chicken livers and dry off, then cut into small pieces. Add to the onions with the bacon, if used, and cook gently for about 10 minutes, stirring from time to time to prevent sticking. Season well, add the wine and allspice and continue cooking for a couple of minutes longer. Remove from the heat, cool a little then mix in the cream. Purée the pâté in a blender or food processor and then adjust the seasonings. Turn into a dish or 6 individual pots and chill. Cover with a little melted butter and garnish with capers and bay leaves which will then set into the butter. Chill until required.

Freezing recommended: for up to 2 months

Avocado and Melon with Raspberry Vinaigrette

Slices of avocado and melon dressed with a raspberry vinaigrette made from fresh raspberries.

Serves 4

2 ripe avocados
1 tablespoon lemon juice
½ small melon (Charantais or Ogen for
preference)

Raspberry Vinaigrette:
75 g (3 oz) raspberries, fresh or frozen

4 tablespoons oil
1 tablespoon white wine vinegar
1 teaspoon lemon juice
1 level teaspoon caster sugar
salt and pepper

Preparation time: 25 minutes

Put the raspberries into a bowl and add all the other dressing ingredients. Mash well together and leave to stand for 30 minutes or so. Then blend the dressing and sieve to remove the pips. Put into a bowl. Just before serving, peel, quarter and slice the avocados and dip in lemon juice. Peel and slice the melon or, if preferred, cut into melon balls using a melon baller. Spoon a thin layer of raspberry vinaigrette onto 4 plates and arrange the slices of avocado and melon on the sauce. Serve any extra dressing separately.

Marinated Mushrooms

Ideal as a starter, this dish must be made at least 24 **hours in** advance to be at its best.

Serves 6

1 clove garlic, crushed
1 onion, peeled and finely chopped
2 tablespoons oil
150 ml (¼ pint) wine vinegar
1 tablespoon clear honey
½ level teaspoon French mustard
½ level teaspoon dry mustard

salt and pepper
450 g (1 lb) button mushrooms
8–12 black olives, stoned and halved
2–4 tomatoes, peeled, deseeded and cut
into strips
1 level tablespoon freshly chopped basil
or parsley to garnish

Preparation time: 25 minutes, plus marinating time

Fry the garlic and onion very gently in the oil until soft but not coloured, then remove from the heat. Add the vinegar, honey, mustards and seasonings and bring to the boil. Simmer for 3–4 minutes then remove from the heat. Trim and wipe the mushrooms then place them in a bowl; pour the marinade over and toss well. Cover and leave for at least 12 hours, giving an occasional stir. Before serving, add the olives and tomato strips and toss together. Serve individually in small bowls, sprinkled generously with chopped fresh basil or parsley, with warm crusty bread.

Unsuitable for freezing but will keep in the refrigerator for up to 4 days.

23

Spinach Roulade

This is much easier to make than you might think; and the fillings can be widely varied from the basic chicken one.

Serves 8

450 g (1 lb) frozen or 900 g (2 lb) fresh
   spinach (350 g/12 oz after cooking
   and draining)
3 level tablespoons natural yogurt or
   soured cream

salt and pepper
¼ level teaspoon ground nutmeg
4–5 eggs, separated

Filling:
40 g (1½ oz) butter or margarine
300 g (10 oz) raw chicken breast or
   thigh, cut into strips
6–8 spring onions, trimmed and sliced
75 g (3 oz) button mushrooms, sliced
50 g (2 oz) walnut halves, roughly
   chopped

150 ml (¼ pint) natural yogurt
1 level teaspoon cornflour
2 tablespoons water
good dash of Worcestershire sauce
2 hard–boiled eggs, roughly chopped
2 level tablespoons grated Parmesan
   cheese

Preparation time: *30 minutes*
Cooking time: *30 minutes*
Heat the oven to 200°C/400°F/Gas Mark 6.

Line a swiss roll tin approx 33 x 23 cm (13 x 9 inches) with non–stick silicone paper. Cook the spinach and squeeze out as much moisture as possible, using a potato masher. Chop very finely, then beat in the yogurt, seasonings, nutmeg and egg yolks until smoothly blended. Whisk the egg whites until very stiff and standing in peaks. Beat 2 tablespoons of egg white into the spinach and then carefully and evenly fold in the remainder. Pour into the tin and spread out evenly. Cook in a fairly hot oven for 15–20 minutes until set.

Meanwhile melt the fat in a frying pan and sauté the strips of chicken until well sealed. Add the onions and mushrooms and continue for 4–5 minutes until the chicken is cooked through. Stir in the nuts and season well. Blend the yogurt with the cornflour and water, add to the pan and bring slowly to the boil, stirring continuously. Add the Worcestershire sauce and eggs and heat gently.

Turn the spinach roulade onto a sheet of non–stick silicone paper dredged with half the Parmesan cheese and peel off the cooking paper. Spoon the chicken filling evenly over it immediately, then roll up carefully with the help of the paper. Transfer to a serving dish, sprinkle with the remaining cheese and return to the oven for a few minutes. Serve hot, in slices.

LIGHT MEALS, SNACKS AND PASTA

INTRODUCTION

In this age of rushing about it is often necessary to serve meals quickly and at varying times in order to keep the family fed properly. Light meals and snacks form a very important part of the diet so need to be substantial enough to satisfy, with a good nutritional value, and must be the type of dish that is not going to spoil if served later than expected.

Pastry dishes and pasta dishes easily fit the bill and will not keep the poor cook tied to the kitchen for hours on end. Quiches and flans are good served hot, warm or cold, as are pasties, pies and pizzas; and they can be reheated in a moderate oven or microwave as and when required.

Pasta is always quick to cook but it is often the sauce to accompany it that takes the time to prepare and this can always be made in advance, with the pasta being cooked just before eating. Remember, too, that many different types of pasta are interchangeable in the recipes and the plain varieties can be replaced by either the green (spinach flavoured), orange (tomato flavoured) or brown (wholewheat) to widen the choice further. Fresh pasta, which is also widely available in pasta shops and most supermarkets, is delicious and it only takes about 5 minutes to cook; definitely worth a try at some stage. Larger quantities can easily be made and split into individual containers, or enough for two to be served when required, or frozen for use at a later date.

Filled rolls, split and filled French bread or pitta bread are all useful additions to the light meals and snacks repertoire and are also useful for packed lunches and picnics. Vary fillings basing them on meat, fish, pâté, cheese or egg, and add something interesting too, such as lettuce and sliced pear; cucumber, cress and chopped nuts; beetroot and grated apple. These can be prepared and wrapped the night before, provided they are stored in the refrigerator. Slices of quiche, sausagemeat nuggets, cheese and bacon granary bars and potted meats are all recipes that can be used for packed lunches. Remember to complete the meal or snack with a piece of fruit and a tomato or a few sticks of raw celery and carrots.

Shortcrust Pastry

The basic pastry recipe forms a part of so many recipes both sweet and savoury. Plain white flour can be replaced completely or partly by a brown (wholemeal or wholewheat) flour or granary flour. Only sift white flour or you will sift out all the interesting 'bits and pieces'.

225 g (8 oz) plain flour
good pinch of salt
50 g (2 oz) butter or block margarine

50 g (2 oz) lard or white fat
approx 4 tablespoons cold water to mix

Preparation time: *15 minutes*

Sift the flour and salt into a bowl. Add the fats cut into small pieces and rub in with the fingertips until the mixture resembles fine breadcrumbs. This stage can be done in a food processor or electric mixer fitted with a dough hook. Add sufficient water to mix to a firm but pliable dough, using a round–bladed knife or a fork. Knead very lightly then turn onto a lightly floured surface ready for rolling. If time allows, wrap and chill for 30 minutes before rolling out.

Note: pastries are usually measured by their weight of flour eg. 225 g (8 oz) shortcrust pastry is made using 225 g (8 oz) flour etc.

Variations: wholemeal pastry requires a little more water to mix.

Cheese pastry – add a good pinch of cayenne pepper and/or ½ level teaspoon dry mustard and 50 g (2 oz) mature Cheddar cheese, finely grated and 1 level tablespoon grated Parmesan cheese.

Curry pastry – add 1–2 level teaspoons curry powder to the dry ingredients.

Herb pastry – add 1½–2 level teaspoons any dried herbs to the dry ingredients.

Poacher's Roll

A delicious pie which will be well received on a great many occasions.

Serves 8

450 g (1 lb) sausagemeat without herbs
1 onion, peeled and very finely chopped
175 g (6 oz) lean bacon, derinded and
  chopped
¾ level teaspoon dried sage

75 g (3 oz) mushrooms, chopped
salt and pepper
about 350 g (12 oz) made puff pastry
  (thawed if frozen)
beaten egg or top of the milk to glaze

Preparation time: *20 minutes*
Cooking time: *1 hour*
Heat the oven to 200°C/400°F/Gas mark 6.

Combine the sausagemeat, onion, bacon, sage, mushrooms and seasonings and form into a brick shape about 20 x 7.5 cm (8 x 3 inches). Roll out the pastry on a floured surface until it is large enough to enclose the sausage-meat easily. Stand the sausagemeat brick in the centre of the pastry and fold the sides over and the ends in to completely cover it, sealing with beaten egg or milk. Turn the roll over so the joins are underneath and stand on a lightly greased baking sheet. Brush all over with beaten egg, decorate the top with leaves made from the pastry trimmings, then glaze again and make one or two slits in the top for the steam to escape. Cook in a fairly hot oven for 25 minutes. Reduce the temperature to moderate (180°C/350°F/Gas mark 4) and continue to cook for about 20 minutes, laying a sheet of greaseproof paper over the top when it is sufficiently browned. Leave to cool then chill. Serve in slices with salads. Ideal to take on a picnic.

Freezing recommended: *for up to 2 months.*

Blue Cheese Quiche

Use any type of blue hard cheese such as Stilton, Danish Blue, Shropshire Blue etc., for this quiche which can be served hot or cold.

Serves 5–6

175 g (6 oz) shortcrust pastry (see basic recipe, page 26)
Filling:
6 spring onions, trimmed and thinly sliced
175 g (6 oz) blue cheese, rind removed and crumbled or coarsely grated
3 eggs (size 2 or 3)
150 ml (¼ pint) single cream
150 ml (¼ pint) milk

3–4 tablespoons soured cream or natural yogurt
salt and pepper
good pinch of ground nutmeg or allspice
40 g (1½ oz) Cheddar cheese, grated

To garnish:
spring onions
radishes
cucumber slices

Preparation time: *20 minutes*
Cooking time: *45 minutes*
Heat the oven to 220°C/425°F/Gas mark 7.

Make up pastry and use to line a flan ring, dish or tin approx 23 cm (9 inches) in diameter. Sprinkle the onions in the base then add the crumbled blue cheese. Beat the eggs together then gradually beat in the cream, milk and soured cream or yogurt. Season well with salt, pepper and nutmeg or allspice and pour into the pastry case. Sprinkle with the Cheddar cheese and bake in a hot oven for 20 minutes. Reduce the temperature to moderate (180°C/350°F/Gas mark 4) and continue for 20–25 minutes or until set and golden brown. Serve hot or cold, garnished with spring onions, radishes and slices of cucumber.

Freezing recommended: *for up to 2 months*

Baked Mushrooms

These large mushrooms with a filling of spinach and salami make a good quick and easy lunch or supper dish.

Serves 4

8 large open–cup or flat mushrooms
little oil
100 g (4 oz) chopped spinach
40 g (1½ oz) salami, chopped
50 g (2 oz) cream cheese
salt and pepper

little ground coriander
1 egg yolk
1 level tablespoon grated Parmesan
  cheese
25 g (1 oz) fresh breadcrumbs

Preparation time: *20 minutes*
Cooking time: *20–25 minutes*
Heat the oven to 200°C/400°F/Gas mark 6.

Trim and wipe the mushrooms and brush lightly all over with oil. Stand them in an ovenproof dish. Combine the spinach, salami, cream cheese, seasonings, coriander and egg yolk and divide between the mushrooms, pressing the stuffing evenly around the stalk. Combine the Parmesan cheese and breadcrumbs and sprinkle over the filled mushrooms. Cook uncovered, in a fairly hot oven for about 20 minutes. Serve at once.

Hot Cheese Soufflé and Variations

The basic soufflé recipe to which other ingredients can be added, to create a dish suitable for serving at various times and occasions. Remember to eat it straight from the oven or it will sink before your eyes.

Serves 3–4

3 eggs (size 2), separated
25 g (1 oz) butter or margarine
25 g (1 oz) flour
150 ml (¼ pint) milk
salt and pepper

½ level teaspoon English or French
  mustard
75 g (3 oz) mature Cheddar cheese,
  finely grated
2 level tablespoons grated Parmesan
  cheese

Preparation time: *30 minutes*
Cooking time: *35–40 minutes*
Heat the oven to 200°C/400°F/Gas mark 6.

Grease an 18 cm (7 inch) soufflé dish. Separate the eggs, putting the whites into a large grease–free bowl. Melt the fat in a saucepan (not too small or there will not be room to fold in the egg whites). Stir in the flour and cook for a minute or two, stirring all the time. Gradually add the milk, stirring continuously, and bring to the boil. Remove from the heat and beat in the seasonings, mustard and cheese, followed by the egg yolks, one at a time. Whisk the

28

egg whites until very stiff and standing in peaks. Beat two tablespoons of the egg white into the sauce and then quickly fold in the remainder using a metal spoon or plastic spatula. Pour at once into the soufflé dish and cook immediately in a fairly hot oven for about 35 minutes or until well risen and brown. Do not be tempted to look in the oven for the first 30 minutes or the soufflé will sink, and when you do look, close the door very carefully for a sudden jolt or blast of cool air can also cause it to sink. Serve immediately it is ready.

Variations:

Smoked fish – finely flake 75 g (3 oz) cooked or canned smoked fish e.g. kippers, smoked mackerel, smoked haddock or smoked salmon and add to the sauce in place of the cheese. Omit the mustard and add 1–2 level tablespoons freshly chopped parsley or 1 level tablespoon finely chopped chives.

Tomato and Sweetcorn – fry 1 large sliced onion in a little oil until soft, add 3–4 peeled and sliced tomatoes, a 200 g (7 oz) can sweetcorn, seasonings and a few herbs. Cook gently for 2–3 minutes then pour into a 20 cm (8 inch) soufflé dish. Make up the basic cheese soufflé mixture and pour over the tomato mixture, cook as above but it will need approx. 5 minutes longer.

Cheese and Bacon Granary Bars

These crunchy scone bars filled with cream cheese and salad make an excellent snack.

Makes 6

150 g (5 oz) granary flour
150 g (5 oz) self–raising flour
good pinch of salt
2 level teaspoons baking powder
40 g (1½ oz) butter or margarine
1 level teaspoon dried oregano, marjoram or thyme
75 g (3 oz) lean bacon, very finely chopped or minced
75 g (3 oz) onion, very finely chopped or minced

1–2 level tablespoons grated Parmesan cheese
50 g (2 oz) mature Cheddar or Gruyère cheese, grated
approx. 150 ml (¼ pint) milk, fresh or sour
1 tablespoon lemon juice

Filling: *crispy lettuce*
sliced cucumber and/or spring onions
cream cheese, cottage cheese or any spreading cheese

Preparation time: *25 minutes*
Cooking time: *30 minutes*
Heat the oven to 220°C/425°F/Gas mark 7.

Put the granary flour into a bowl and sift in the self–raising flour, salt and baking powder. Rub in the fat finely, then add the herbs. Cook the bacon and the onion together in a small pan with no added fat for 3–4 minutes, then strain and leave to cool. Mix evenly into the dry ingredients with the grated cheeses and bind to a softish dough with the milk and lemon juice combined. Knead lightly and shape into a bar of approx. 25 x 12.5 cm (10 x 5 inches). Place on a well–floured baking sheet and mark into 6 bars. Cook in a hot oven for about 25–30 minutes until well risen, golden brown and firm to the touch. Cool, cut into bars, split open and fill with cheese and salad.

Note: for vegetarians the bacon may be omitted; fry the onion in a little oil.

Potted Meat

An excellent way to use the leftovers of any joint, chicken, turkey or game.

Serves 4–6

225 g (8 oz) cooked turkey, chicken, pork,
    beef, ham, lamb or any game meat
100 g (4 oz) butter
1 onion, peeled and very finely chopped
1–2 cloves garlic, crushed
2 tablespoons sherry

little stock
salt and freshly ground black pepper
good pinch of ground mace, nutmeg or
    coriander

To garnish:
cucumber and tomato slices

Preparation time: *20–25 minutes*

Mince the meat finely or chop finely in a food processor. Melt half the butter in a pan and fry the onion and garlic very gently until soft but not coloured. Stir in the minced meat, mixing thoroughly, then add the sherry and sufficient stock to moisten. Remove from the heat and season well with salt, pepper and mace or other spice. Press into a lightly greased container or several individual pots and level the tops. Chill until firm.

Melt the remaining butter and pour in an even layer over the potted meat. Chill until required. Garnish with cucumber and tomato and serve with fresh crusty bread, rolls, toast or crispbread and salads. Can be stored in the refrigerator for 2–3 days only since it does not contain preservatives.

Savoury Gougère

Choux pastry makes a delicious ring to fill with a variety of savoury fillings.

Serves 4

Choux Pastry:
50 g (2 oz) butter
150 ml (¼ pint) water
65 g (2½ oz) plain flour, sifted
pinch of salt (optional)
2 eggs (size 3 or 4), beaten

Filling:
50 g (2 oz) butter or margarine
1 onion, peeled and thinly sliced
1 clove garlic, crushed
1 green pepper, deseeded and chopped
100 g (4 oz) mushrooms, sliced

40 g (1½ oz) flour
150 ml (¼ pint) cider or dry white wine
150 ml (¼ pint) milk
salt and pepper
½ level teaspoon made mustard

2 level tablespoons grated Parmesan
  cheese
225 g (8 oz) cooked ham, chopped or cut
  into strips
25 g (1 oz) Cheddar cheese grated

Preparation time: 40 minutes
Cooking time: 45 minutes
Heat the oven to 220°C/425°F/Gas mark 7.

For the gougère: melt the butter in the water in a saucepan and bring to the boil. Add the flour all at once and beat hard until it forms a ball and leaves the sides of the pan clean. Remove from the heat, add the salt, if used, and beat until quite smooth. Spread out over the base of the pan and leave to cool for 5–10 minutes. Gradually beat in the beaten eggs about 2 teaspoons at a time, preferably using a hand–held electric mixer and making sure the egg is completely incorporated before adding more. Continue until the mixture is smooth and glossy and holds its shape. Sometimes it will not quite take all the egg. Put the choux paste into a piping bag fitted with a large plain vegetable nozzle and pipe into a ring 21–23 cm (8–9 inches) in diameter on a greased baking sheet. Alternatively simply spoon and spread the paste to form the ring. Cook in a hot oven for about 40 minutes or until well risen, firm to the touch and golden brown. Make a slit or two in the sides of the ring for the steam to escape and return to the oven for a couple of minutes to dry out.

For the filling: melt the fat in a pan and fry the onion and garlic very gently until soft. Add the pepper and continue frying for 2–3 minutes, then add the mushrooms and cook briefly. Stir in the flour and cook for a minute or so and then gradually add the cider or wine and milk and bring to the boil, stirring continuously. The sauce should be fairly thick. Season well and stir in the mustard followed by the cheese and ham. Heat through until really hot. Cut the top one–third off the gougère and scoop out any uncooked dough. Spoon in the filling, replace the lid and sprinkle with Cheddar cheese. Return to the oven for 3–4 minutes to melt the cheese. Serve hot.

Chinese Egg Rolls

The interest in these has grown with the popularity of Chinese foods. They are really very simple to make.

Serves 6–8 (makes 12–16 rolls).

100 g (4 oz) plain flour
2 level tablespoons cornflour
good pinch of salt
2 eggs (size 2 or 3) lightly beaten
400ml (14 fl oz) water

deep fat or oil for frying

Filling:
50 g (2 oz) peeled prawns
50 g (2 oz) celery, finely chopped

75 g (3 oz) cooked pork or chicken,
  minced
75 g (3 oz) canned water chestnuts,
  very finely chopped
75 g (3 oz) canned bamboo shoots, very
  finely chopped
2–3 teaspoons dry sherry

1 tablespoon soy sauce
1 level tablespoon very finely chopped
  spring onion or onion
1 egg
salt and pepper

To garnish:
spring onion flowers

Preparation time: *40 minutes, plus chilling time*
Cooking time: *15 minutes*

For the pancakes: sift the flour, cornflour and salt into a bowl and gradually beat in the eggs and water to give a smooth batter as thin as cream. Cook the pancakes in a heavy based pan lightly greased with oil or lard for 1–2 minutes until set and lightly browned Do not cook the second side but cool on wire racks and then stack in layers with discs of greaseproof or non–stick paper between them. *For the filling:* combine all the ingredients, adding seasonings to taste and form into finger–shaped rolls. Put a roll of filling on the cooked side of a pancake, fold in the ends and roll up evenly, sealing the edges with a little uncooked batter or beaten egg. Fill the others in the same way then chill for 2–3 hours.

  To serve: heat the fat or oil until a cube of bread browns in 60 seconds. Deep fry the egg rolls, three or four at a time until golden brown all over. Drain on absorbent kitchen paper and keep warm whilst frying the remainder. Serve garnished with spring onion 'flowers' and accompanied by bowls of soy sauce and/or chilli sauce.

Spring Onion Flowers

Remove the root from the spring onions and trim to about 7.5 cm (3 inches). Cut lengthwise through the stalk several times to within 4 cm (1 ½ inches) of the base end. Place in iced water for about an hour to open out. Drain and use.

Sausage Tattie 'Ash

This is a dish taken from the North, just right for the cold weather.

Serves 4–5

450 g (1 lb) chipolata sausages
1 tablespoon oil
1–2 onions, peeled and sliced
450 g (1 lb) small new potatoes
  or 675 g (1½ lb) old potatoes
225 g (½ lb) small carrots, peeled and
  sliced
2 leeks, trimmed, sliced and washed

1 parsnip, peeled and roughly diced
salt and pepper
1 teaspoon Worcestershire sauce
1 teaspoon mushroom ketchup
  or curry powder (optional)
450 ml (¾ pint) beef stock
freshly chopped parsley to garnish

Preparation time: *20 minutes*
Cooking time: *1–1¼ hours*
Heat the oven to 180°C/350°F/Gas mark 4.

Halve the chipolatas by first twisting each in half in the centre and then cutting. Fry in the oil to just brown and transfer to a casserole. Fry the onions in the same oil until lightly browned then add to the casserole. New potatoes may be left in their skins or peeled, and if large cut in half. With old potatoes, peel and cut into large chunks and add to the casserole. Mix in the carrots, leeks and parsnip and season well. Mix the Worcestershire sauce and ketchup or curry powder with the stock, bring to the boil and pour into the casserole. Cover tightly and cook in a moderate oven for 1–1¼ hours or until very tender. Serve piping hot sprinkled liberally with irsley.

ote: any type of sausages may be used for this dish but cut them in half or into thirds before adding to the dish. With non–herbed varieties, 1 level teaspoon mixed herbs or oregano may be added to the casserole.

Pasta Beanpot

A good vegetarian mixture of pasta, beans and vegetables topped with cheese.

Serves 5–6

225 g (8 oz) pasta twists or shells
salt and pepper
1 large onion, peeled and sliced
2 carrots, peeled and chopped
1 clove garlic, crushed
2 tablespoons oil
1–2 leeks, trimmed and sliced
425 g (15 oz) can red kidney beans, drained

200 g (7 oz) can sweet corn kernels
75 g (3 oz) shelled walnuts or pecan nuts, roughly chopped
150 ml (¼ pint) white wine, cider or stock
50 g (2 oz) mature Cheddar cheese, grated

Preparation time: *30 minutes*
Cooking time: *20 minutes*

Cook the pasta in plenty of boiling salted water until barely tender, about 8–9 minutes. Drain thoroughly. Meanwhile fry the onion, carrots and garlic in the oil until soft but only lightly coloured. Add the leeks and continue for a few minutes longer. Add the beans, sweet corn, nuts, wine, cider or stock and seasonings and bring to the boil. Add the pasta to the pan and simmer gently for 3–4 minutes until really hot. Adjust the seasonings and turn into a flameproof dish. Sprinkle with the cheese and put under a moderate grill until golden brown. Serve at once.

Cartwheel Salad

Pasta shapes mixed with grapes, bacon, chicken, carrots and peas to give a colourful and tasty salad.

Serves 4

225 g (8 oz) pasta wheels or spirals (or other similar shapes)
½ bunch spring onion, trimmed and sliced
or 1 level tablespoon freshly chopped parsley
100 g (4 oz) seedless green grapes or large grapes, halved and depipped
100 g (4 oz) streaky bacon, crisply fried and roughly chopped
225 g (8 oz) cooked chicken or turkey meat, cut into strips

a few black olives
2 carrots, peeled and cut into narrow sticks
100 g (4 oz) cooked peas

Creamy Dressing:
6 tablespoons French dressing
2 tablespoons cream, single or double
½ level teaspoon coarse grain mustard
salt and pepper
lettuce and/or watercress

Preparation time: 25 minutes

Cook the pasta wheels or spirals until *al dente* (still with a slight bite in it) in boiling water for about 12 minutes; then drain thoroughly. Cool. Put all the other ingredients into a mixing bowl and mix lightly. Whisk the French dressing and other dressing ingredients together and season well. Pour over the salad, add the pasta and toss together lightly but thoroughly. Serve on a platter on a bed of lettuce or watercress.

Noodles With Ham and Raisins

Ham, raisins and mushrooms in a creamy sauce to serve on noodles or spaghetti.

Serves 4

225 g (8 oz) thin noodles or spaghetti
25 g (1 oz) butter or margarine
1 tablespoon oil
1 onion, peeled and chopped
1 clove garlic, crushed
100 g (4 oz) mushrooms, trimmed and sliced
50 g (2 oz) raisins

150 ml (¼ pint) soured cream or natural yogurt
175 g (6 oz) cooked ham, chopped
1 peperami sausage, thinly sliced
salt and pepper
1 level tablespoon freshly chopped mint or parsley

Preparation time: 20 minutes
Cooking time: 20 minutes

Cook the noodles in plenty of boiling salted water, following the instructions on the packet, or for about 9 minutes. Spaghetti will take a couple of minutes longer. If using fresh pasta (see below) you will need only 3–4 minutes' cooking. Drain well. Meanwhile heat the butter and oil in a pan and fry the onion and garlic gently until soft. Add the mushrooms and continue for a minute or so, then add the raisins, soured cream or yogurt, ham and peperami and bring to the boil. Simmer gently for 2–3 minutes, season to taste and stir in the parsley. Either toss the mixture through the noodles or spaghetti or serve spooned on to a bed of noodles.

Note: if buying fresh pasta from a supermarket or pasta shop it is often possible to obtain a mixture of spinach and egg noodles which provide two colours and flavours to add extra interest to the dish.

Bacon and Bean Lasagne

The red beans in this recipe can be interchanged with flageolet, borlini, cannelini beans or even chick peas.

Serves 4–6

6–8 sheets lasagne, green or white
salt and pepper
3 tablespoons oil
1 large onion, peeled and thinly sliced
2–3 carrots, peeled and chopped
2 sticks celery, sliced (optional)
1 clove garlic, crushed
100–175 g (4–6 oz) bacon, derinded and
  chopped
225 g (8 oz) baked beans
225 g (8 oz) can peeled tomatoes
425 g (15 oz) can red kidney beans,
  drained
1 level tablespoon tomato purée
½ teaspoon Worcestershire sauce

¾ level teaspoon dried oregano or
  marjoram

Sauce:
40 g (1½ oz) butter or margarine
40 g (1½ oz) flour
450 ml (¾ pint) milk
½ level teaspoon made mustard
salt and pepper
2 hard–boiled eggs, sliced
50 g (2 oz) mature Cheddar cheese,
  grated
or 2 level tablespoons grated Parmesan
  cheese

Preparation time: *45 minutes*
Cooking time: *45 minutes*
Heat the oven to 200°C/400°F/Gas mark 6.

Cook the lasagne, a few sheets at a time until tender, in boiling salt water with 1 tablespoon oil added; drain on absorbent kitchen paper. (Check that your type of lasagne needs pre–cooking; some varieties do not). Fry the onion, carrots, and celery and garlic in 2 tablespoons oil until soft (about 5 minutes), add the bacon and continue for 3–5 minutes. Pour off any excess fat from the pan then add the baked beans, tomatoes, red beans and tomato purée. Bring to the boil and simmer for about 5 minutes. Season well and add the Worcestershire sauce and herbs.

Use the fat, flour and milk to make a white sauce and stir in the mustard and seasonings to taste. If you prefer the sauce thinner, you can add up to 150 ml (¼ pint) extra milk. In a greased ovenproof dish alternate layers of lasagne with the bacon mixture and most of the white sauce. Arrange rows of sliced egg on top and cover with the rest of the white sauce. Sprinkle with cheese and cook in a fairly hot oven for 30–40 minutes until browned and bubbling.

Vegetable Pasta Bake

A delicious vegetarian pasta dish or good accompaniment to grills, chops, or sausages.

Serves 4

225 g (8 oz) short cut macaroni or other
   similar sized pasta shapes
salt and pepper
oil
65 g (2½ oz) butter or margarine
40 g (1½ oz) flour
450 ml (¾ pint) milk
100 g (4 oz) mature Cheddar cheese,
   grated
½ level teaspoon dry mustard

1–2 cloves garlic
3 carrots, peeled and diced
1 red pepper, deseeded and sliced
2 large courgettes, trimmed and thinly
   sliced
100 g (4 oz) mushrooms, sliced

To garnish:
slices of tomato and raw courgette or
   cucumber

Preparation time: *20 minutes*
Cooking time: *45 minutes*
Heat the oven to 200°C/400°F/Gas mark 6.

Cook the macaroni in boiling salted water with 1 tablespoon oil added, until barely tender. Drain immediately and rinse under cold water. Melt 40 g (1½ oz) fat in a pan, stir in the flour and cook for a minute or so. Gradually add the milk and bring to the boil, stirring frequently until thickened. Stir in just over half the cheese, the mustard and seasonings to taste. Melt the remaining fat with 1 tablespoon oil in a pan and add the garlic and carrots. Fry gently for 3–4 minutes then add the pepper and continue for 2 minutes. Add the courgettes and mushrooms and cook for a further couple of minutes, stirring frequently; season to taste. Put half the macaroni in a greased ovenproof dish and cover with the vegetable mixture and about a third of the sauce. Cover with the remaining macaroni then the rest of the sauce. Sprinkle with the reserved cheese and cook in a fairly hot oven for 30–40 minutes until bubbling and browned. Garnish with slices of tomato and raw courgette and serve at once.

Note: the vegetable mixture can be varied to suit your taste and what is available.

VEGETABLES AND SALADS

INTRODUCTION

Vegetables, particularly salads, play a much more important part in our diet than they used to. The meat and two veg traditionally served by every-one ensured that vegetables were eaten, but nowadays these 'two veg' are much more interesting and probably better cooked. In fact, with the wide–spread swing to healthier eating and the increased number of vege-tarians, a whole wealth of adventurous ways of serving vegetables has been devised, quite a number of which can form the main part of the meal. The great variety of 'unusual' vegetables which are imported into the country have now become commonplace alongside all the old favourites.

When it comes to salads, freshness and crispness are the most important factors; limp and stale produce does not make either an attractive presenta-tion or set anyone's taste buds alive. Salad accompaniments should have only a few ingredients but main course ones can be hearty with a good selection of components. A salad needs a good dressing. These are simply made and can be varied by using different oils and vinegars, of which there is now a good selection in the supermarkets. Do not add the dressing to the salad too soon or it will saturate and spoil the ingredients; although some specified salads and vegetables do benefit from marinating in place of part or all of the cooking.

All vegetables and salads are high in vitamins B and C, with a good supply of carotene, iron and calcium, and contain plenty of fibre, particu-larly when cooked and eaten in their skins. Green leafy vegetables, salads and potatoes are higher in vitamin C than root vegetables. Take care to peel thinly for the most valuable nutrients are found immediately beneath the skin.

Always cook vegetables in the minimum of water and until they are only just tender. Over–cooking drains all the nutrients into the cooking water and leaves the vegetables flabby and uninteresting. Add salt sparingly if liked, and serve as soon as possible after cooking. However, vegetables can be reheated successfully in the microwave after cooking earlier in the day. Cover and allow about 2 minutes.

Buy both vegetables and salad stuffs regularly and store vegetables in a cool dark place and salads in the crisper of the refrigerator. If vegetables are bought in polythene bags, either take them out or make large holes in the bag for ventilation. Paper bags are best for storing vegetables as they are porous and do not cause sweating. Don't wash vegetables or salads until required, as if they are stored wet they will simply go soggy and mouldy and last a very short time.

Potato Galette with Chives

A delicious potato cake from France which can also utilize mashed potato or the insides of jacket potatoes when the skins are required elsewhere.

Serves 5–6

6 large baking potatoes
100 g (4 oz) butter
3 onions, peeled and thinly sliced
salt and black pepper

good pinch of ground mace, nutmeg or
  coriander
3–4 tablespoons freshly chopped chives

Preparation time: 20 minutes
Cooking time: 1¼–½ hours
Heat the oven to 220°C/425°F/Gas mark 7.

Bake the potatoes in a fairly hot oven for about an hour or until soft. Cool slightly, split open and scoop out the flesh. Melt about 25 g (1 oz) butter in a pan and fry the onions very gently until soft, but only barely coloured – this will take at least 10 minutes. Mash the potato flesh whilst the onions cook. Add about half the remaining butter to the onions and when melted, add the potato, seasonings, mace or coriander and half the chives. Stir the mixture so the onions are evenly incorporated then smooth out until even in the pan. Turn the grill on to moderate. Cook the potato cake over low heat for 4–5 minutes until browning underneath, then dot the top with the remaining butter and place under the grill for a few minutes until evenly browned. Carefully slide onto a plate, sprinkle with the remaining chives and serve cut into wedges.

Mushroom and Sesame Stir–fry

Stir–fries are quick and easy to prepare and make an excellent vegetable accompaniment or vegetarian main course. Always use very fresh ingredients.

Serves 4

2 tablespoons oil
1 small onion, peeled and very finely
  sliced
2 carrots, peeled and cut into narrow
  sticks
2 sticks celery, cut into narrow sticks
1 red pepper, deseeded and thinly sliced

2 courgettes, trimmed and thinly sliced
225 g (8 oz) button mushrooms,
  quartered or sliced
2 tablespoons light soy sauce
1 tablespoon lemon juice
1 tablespoon wine vinegar
1 level tablespoon sesame seeds

Preparation time: 20 minutes
Cooking time: 10 minutes

Heat the oil in a wok or large frying pan and fry the onion quickly for 2 minutes. Add the carrots and celery and continue cooking for a further 2 minutes. Toss in the pepper and courgettes and continue again for about 2 minutes, stirring frequently. Add the mushrooms, soy sauce, lemon juice and vinegar, toss thoroughly and cook for a further 2 minutes. Season to taste and serve hot, liberally sprinkled with sesame seeds.

Boston Baked Beans

The long slow cooking is necessary to give the true flavour to this dish; it can be cooked overnight for 8 hours in a slightly cooler oven.

Serves 4

350 g (¾ lb) haricot beans
2 tablespoons black treacle
2 tablespoons tomato ketchup
1 level tablespoon dry mustard
2 level teaspoons salt
black pepper
½ teaspoon Worcestershire sauce

2 tablespoons wine or cider vinegar
1 level teaspoon demerara sugar
2 onions, peeled and chopped
6 whole cloves
4–5 thick slices belly pork (fresh or
  salted), skinned

Preparation time: 20 minutes
Cooking time: 6 hours
Heat the oven to 150°C/300°F/Gas Mark 2.

Wash the beans thoroughly then soak in fresh cold water overnight, if time allows. Drain and rinse and place the beans in a saucepan, cover with cold water and bring to the boil. Cook for 30 minutes then drain, reserving the liquor. Place the beans in a heavy ovenproof casserole and stir in the treacle, ketchup, mustard, salt, plenty of pepper, Worcestershire sauce, vinegar, sugar, onions and cloves. Cut the pork into 2.5 cm (1 inch) pieces and add to the beans with about 300 ml (½ pint) bean liquor. Cover very tightly and cook in a slow oven for about 6 hours. The pork should have merged into the beans. Discard cloves and serve with wholemeal or rye bread and a salad; or just by itself.

VEGETABLE COOKING CHART

VEGETABLE	BOILING	ROASTING	STEAMING	BAKING OR BRAISING	FRYING
Potatoes	Old 20–30 mins New 15–20 mins	200–220°C/200–220F° Gas Mark 6–7 For about an hour	Small new or diced old for about 30 mins	In skins and pricked all over. As for roasting	Chipped or sliced Deep fat or oil at 190°C/375°F for 6–7 mins
Parsnips	20–30 minutes	As for potatoes			
Leeks	Sliced 5–10 mins Whole 12–15 mins			With butter and stock, covered at 180°C/350°F, Gas Mark 4 40–50 mins.	
Carrots	New 12–15 mins Old 10–15 mins Diced 5–10 mins		Sliced or diced about 20 mins		
Beans	5–10 minutes		10–15 mins		
Broccoli	about 5 minutes		15–20 mins		
Brussels Sprouts	5–10 minutes		Small sprouts 12–15 mins		
Green Cabbage	5–10 minutes		10–12 mins		
Red Cabbage	10–12 minutes		15–20 mins	With vinegar etc. 180°C/350°F/Gas Mark 4 covered for 1 hour	

VEGETABLE COOKING CHART

VEGETABLE	BOILING	ROASTING	STEAMING	BAKING OR BRAISING	FRYING
Cauliflower	Whole 15–20 mins Florets 8–10 mins		15 mins only for florets		
Peas	Young 8–10 mins Mature 18–20 mins Mange-tout 3–8 mins		15 mins 10 mins		
Spinach	5–10 mins		10–15 mins		
Courgettes	3–8 mins		5–10 mins	With butter and stock, covered, 180°C/350°F Gas 4 for 40 mins	As potatoes for 3–5 mins
Marrow	10–15 mins		15–20 mins	In foil at 180°C/350°C/Gas Mark 4 for about 1 hour	
Pumpkin	15–20 mins	Around the meat for 40 minutes	20–25 mins		

Nut Burgers

This mixture can also be made into cutlets to serve with a tomato or mushroom sauce.

Serves 4

1 clove garlic, crushed
1 onion, peeled and chopped
25 g (1 oz) butter or margarine
150 ml (¼ pint) stock (preferably
   vegetable)
100 g (4 oz) Brazil nuts, ground
100 g (4 oz) chopped mixed nuts
50 g (2 oz) fresh breadcrumbs

1 level teaspoon freshly chopped parsley
1 level teaspoon dried thyme
salt and pepper
1 level teaspoon vegetable extract
   (Marmite or Vegemite)
4 fresh baps
salads to garnish

Preparation time: 25 minutes
Cooking time: 25–30 minutes
Heat the oven to 180°C/350°F/Gas mark 4.

Fry the garlic and onion in the melted fat until soft, but not coloured. Stir in the flour and cook for a minute or so. Gradually add the stock and bring to the boil. Remove from the heat and stir in the nuts, breadcrumbs, parsley, thyme, salt and pepper and vegetable extract. Leave until cold. Shape into four round burgers or cutlet shapes. Place on a greased baking sheet and cook in a moderate oven for about 25 minutes. Serve in split baps with shredded lettuce, spring onions, sliced tomatoes or other salads. The burgers can also be served cold.

Leek and Onion Tartlets

Simple to make and ideal for packed lunches and picnics as well making a very good vegetarian meal. The mixture can also be made into a 23 cm (9 inch) flan.

Makes 4–5 tartlets

225 g (½ lb) shortcrust pastry (see page
   26)

Filling:
1 large onion, peeled and thinly sliced
1 clove garlic, crushed
2 tablespoons oil
450 g (1 lb) leeks, trimmed and thinly
   sliced

50 g (2 oz) butter or margarine
1 large egg (size 1 or 2)
150 ml (¼ pint) single cream (milk or
   yogurt may be used if preferred)
salt and pepper
good pinch of ground allspice
50 g (2 oz) mature Cheddar cheese,
   finely grated

Preparation time: 25 minutes
Cooking time: 40–45 minutes
Heat the oven to 220°C/425°F/Gas mark 7.

Make up the pastry and chill whilst preparing the filling. Fry the onion and garlic gently in the oil until soft but not coloured. Add the leeks and butter or margarine and continue for 5–6 minutes until the leeks are soft. Cool a little then drain thoroughly in a sieve. Beat the egg and cream together and season well with salt, pepper and allspice.

Roll out the pastry and use to line 4–5 fluted flan tins or individual Yorkshire pudding tins of approx 11 cm (4½ inches) diameter. Divide the leeks and onions between the pastry cases and spoon the egg mixture over each. Sprinkle with cheese and cook in a hot oven for 20 minutes. Reduce to moderate (180°C/350°F/Gas mark 4) and continue for 15–20 minutes until well browned and firm. Serve hot or cold.

Freezing recommended: *for up to 1 month*

Spinach and Walnut Pancakes

An attractive, tasty and nutritious filling to these easy pancakes.

Serves 4 (or 8 as a starter)

Pancake Batter:
100 g (4 oz) plain flour
pinch of salt
1–2 eggs (size 2 or 3)
300 ml (½ pint) milk

Filling:
450 g (1 lb) fresh spinach
3 hard–boiled eggs, chopped
50 g (2 oz) shelled walnuts, chopped
pinch of powdered garlic
½ level teaspoon ground coriander
pinch of ground nutmeg
salt and pepper

4 tablespoons soured cream or yogurt
25 g (1 oz) melted butter

Sauce:
25 g (1 oz) butter or margarine
2 level tablespoons flour
300 ml (½ pint) milk
4 tablespoons soured cream or yogurt
½ level teaspoon dry mustard

Topping:
25 g (1 oz) shelled walnuts, chopped
25–40 g (1–1½ oz) mature Cheddar
  cheese, grated

Preparation time: *30 minutes*
Cooking time: *20–30 minutes*
Heat the oven to 200°C/400°F/Gas mark 6.

For the batter: sift the flour and salt into a bowl and make a well in the centre. Add the egg(s) and a little milk and gradually work in the flour to make a batter, adding more milk as necessary. Beat until smooth then beat in the remaining milk. Use the batter to make 8 pancakes in a 20 cm (8 inch) frying pan and layer up with a piece of greaseproof paper between each one.

For the filling: trim, wash and remove tough stalks from the spinach then cook in the minimum of boiling salted water. Drain very thoroughly and chop finely or purée in a food processor. Place in a bowl with the eggs, walnuts, garlic, coriander, nutmeg and plenty of seasonings. Mix well then bind together with the soured cream and butter. Divide the filling between the pancakes, fold in the sides and roll up to completely enclose. Place in a shallow greased ovenproof dish.

For the sauce: melt the fat in a pan, stir in the flour and cook for a minute or so. Gradually add the milk and bring up to the boil. Simmer for 2 minutes then stir in the cream, mustard and plenty of seasonings. Pour over the pancakes and sprinkle with a mixture of chopped walnuts and grated cheese. Cook in a fairly hot oven for about 30 minutes or until piping hot and browned on top.

Note: a 225g (8 oz) packet frozen chopped spinach may be used in place of fresh spinach.

Basic French Dressing

150 ml (¼ pint) oil (olive, corn, saf-
    flower, sunflower or a combination)
salt and freshly ground black pepper
1–2 cloves garlic, crushed
1 level teaspoon sugar

½ level teaspoon made English mustard
½ level teaspoon French mustard
1 tablespoon lemon juice
approx 1 tablespoon wine or cider
    vinegar

Preparation time: *10 minutes*

Put all the ingredients into a screw–topped jar and shake hard until completely emulsified. Shake hard again before use.

Variations:
Sesame – add 2 level tablespoons sesame seeds.
Herbs – add 2 level tablespoons freshly chopped mixed herbs.
Citrus – add the finely grated rind of 2 limes, 2 lemons or 1 large orange and a little of the juice.
Nut – add 40 g (1½ oz) finely chopped hazelnuts, walnuts, pecans or peanuts.
Tomato – add 1 level tablespoon tomato purée and a few drops of Worcestershire sauce.
Creamy – add 2 tablespoons double cream just before serving.

Mayonnaise

2 egg yolks
¼–½ level teaspoon dry mustard
salt and white pepper
275 ml (scant ½ pint) oil (sunflower,

    vegetable, corn, olive etc.)
2 tablespoons lemon juice
1–2 tablespoons white wine vinegar
1 level teaspoon caster sugar

Preparation time: *20–25 minutes*

You must start with all the ingredients at room temperature – cold eggs or oil will cause curdling. Put the yolks and mustard into a warm bowl, add a touch of salt and pepper and mix thoroughly. Whisk in half the oil, *drop by drop*, until thick, preferably using a hand-held electric mixer or a balloon whisk, then beat in 1 tablespoon lemon juice. Continue to add the rest of the oil, again drop by drop at first, then in a slow trickle. Add the vinegar, more lemon juice to taste and the sugar. Adjust seasonings if necessary. Store in an airtight container or screw–topped jar in the refrigerator for up to 3 weeks.

Note: to make mayonnaise, you need to use raw egg yolks. In view of the recent salmonella in eggs scare you may prefer to use shop bought mayonnaise for the very young or old or those whose health may be at risk.

Variations:
Lemon – substitute lemon juice for the vinegar and add the finely grated rind of 1–2 lemons.
Orange – use half the orange juice in place of the vinegar and add the finely grated rind of 1–2 oranges.
Green – add about 2–3 tablespoons finely chopped parsley or watercress.
Chive – add 3 tablespoons finely chopped chives.
Horseradish – add 1–2 tablespoons horseradish cream or sauce.
Curry – add 2–4 level teaspoons curry powder according to taste.
Brandy or Sherry – replace the vinegar with brandy or sherry.
Cocktail – add 1½–2 tablespoons tomato purée, 1–2 tablespoons tomato ketchup, a good dash of Worcestershire sauce and a dash of lemon juice.
Yogurt – mix equal quantities of mayonnaise with natural yogurt; or soured cream.

Cooked Salad Dressing

Makes approx: 150 ml (¼ pint)

1½ *level tablespoons flour*
1½ *level teaspoons sugar*
1 *level teaspoon dry mustard*
salt and pepper
6 *tablespoons milk*

25 *g (1 oz) butter*
1 *egg (size 2 or 3), beaten*
3–4 *tablespoons vinegar (white wine, cider or tarragon)*
4 *tablespoons oil (any type)*

Preparation time: *10 minutes*
Cooking time: *10 minutes*

Sift the flour and mix with the sugar, mustard, salt and pepper in a small pan. Blend in the milk and bring slowly to the boil, stirring continuously; simmer for 1 minute. Remove from the heat and cool slightly, then beat in the butter followed by the egg. Return to the heat and cook to just below boiling point, stirring all the time, but do not allow to boil. Remove from the heat and gradually beat in the vinegar to taste, followed by the oil. Adjust seasonings, cover tightly and allow to cool. When cold transfer to an airtight container and chill.

Special Potato Salad

This salad is tossed in French dressing with other ingredients, but for the best flavour the potatoes must be hot when they are tossed.

Serves 6

675 g (1½ lb) tiny new potatoes, well
  scrubbed
salt and pepper
150 ml (¼ pint) French dressing (page
  44)
1–2 tablespoons freshly chopped mixed
  herbs

100 g (4 oz) mange–tout, trimmed and
  blanched
1–2 firm courgettes, trimmed and cut
  into thin slanting slices
2 grapefruit, peeled and cut into seg-
  ments, free of white membrane
50 g (2 oz) toasted hazelnuts, chopped

Preparation time: 20 minutes plus cooling time
Cooking time: 20 minutes

If tiny new potatoes are unavailable, use larger ones and when cooked cut into large dice. Cook the potatoes in lightly salted water until just tender; do not overcook. Drain thoroughly and turn into a bowl. Leave to cool for a few minutes then add the herbs and toss evenly in the mixture. Leave until cold. Prepare the mange–tout, courgettes and grapefruit and add to the potatoes, mixing carefully. Turn into a bowl and sprinkle with the hazelnuts. Watercress may be used to garnish, if liked.

Avocado and Egg Salad

This niçoise–style salad makes a good meatless main course or starter.

Serves 4 as a main course, or 6 as a starter

2 ripe avocados
5 tablespoons French dressing (page 44)
2 tablespoons clear honey
1 clove garlic, crushed
crisp lettuce leaves (e.g. Little Gem,
  Iceberg or Webbs)

8–12 cherry tomatoes
1 small onion, peeled and thinly sliced
  1–2 level tablespoons capers, drained
6–8 hard–boiled eggs
12 black olives stoned
1 can anchovy fillets, well drained

Preparation time: 20 minutes

Peel and slice the avocados and place in a bowl. Combine the French dressing, honey and garlic and add to the avocados, tossing well. Tear up the lettuce and put into a small bowl or small dish. Spoon the avocado mixture over the lettuce followed by the tomatoes, onion slices and capers. Peel and quarter the eggs and arrange over the salad. Finally add the olives and anchovies. Serve with crusty bread or rolls.

46

Rosy Red Chicken Salad

A colourful salad with a tangy flavour and plenty of different textures.

Serves 4

50 g (2 oz) radicchio
leaves from ½ feuille de chêne or quattro
    staggione lettuce
1 red onion, peeled and thinly sliced
10–12 radishes, trimmed and quartered
4 stalks celery, cut into short sticks

4–6 tablespoons raspberry dressing (see
    page 22)
225 g (8 oz) cooked chicken breast meat,
    sliced or cut into strips
celery leaves to garnish

Preparation time: 20 minutes

Put all the ingredients for the raspberry dressing into a screw–topped jar (with a few raspberries, if available) and shake until completely emulsified. Tear up the lettuce leaves and mix in a bowl. Add the sliced onion, radishes and celery. Mix and arrange on a serving plate leaving a space down the centre. Drizzle the dressing over the salad. Arrange the chicken slices or strips in the space and garnish with celery leaves.

Leek, Bacon and Pineapple Salad

This makes a good lunch or supper dish or can be served as an accompaniment to grilled meat, fish or poultry.

Serves 4–6

4 leeks, trimmed and thinly sliced
salt and pepper
225 g (8 oz) streaky bacon rashers, rind
    removed
225 g (8 oz) can pineapple rings or
    pieces in natural juice
frisée or curly endive
few radicchio leaves (optional)

1 head chicory
1 green pepper, deseeded and thinly
    sliced
4 tablespoons French dressing (page 44)
1 clove garlic, crushed
1 level tablespoon freshly chopped
    parsley (optional)

Croûtons (page 14)

Preparation time: 25–30 minutes

Blanch the leeks for 2 minutes in boiling water, drain, rinse in cold water and drain again. Fry or grill the bacon until crisp, drain, cool and crumble or roughly chop. Drain the pineapple, reserving 2 tablespoons juice, and cut the remainder into small pieces. Arrange a bed of mixed lettuces and chicory in a shallow bowl. Combine the leeks, pineapple and green pepper and add the dressing, pineapple juice, garlic and parsley (if used). Toss well and spoon onto the salad. Sprinkle with the bacon and croûtons.

FISH

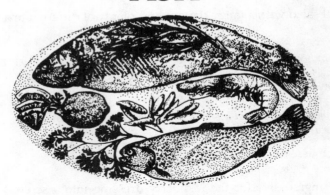

INTRODUCTION

Fish is a very important ingredient in our diet because it has excellent nutritive properties and is easily eaten and digested by people of all ages. There are numerous varieties of fish, both fresh and frozen, which are becoming increasingly available as the larger supermarkets open more and more 'fresh fish' departments alongside their already well stocked compartments of frozen fish and fish products. However, the local fishmonger is the obvious choice if there is one in your area for he has orders of fresh fish delivered daily, making sure it is at its freshest. Frozen food shops also have large fish departments.

Fish can be broken down roughly into three groups – white fish, oily fish and shellfish, all of which have slightly different characteristics. White fish has a white flesh, which is sometimes greyish when raw but turns white when cooked. It has a low fat and high protein content, making it ideal for low fat and low cholesterol diets but it can still provide some of the best and most famous fish dishes served in top restaurants. Oily fish has a darker or coloured flesh, which is high in protein but also higher in fat content, although still far lower than many meats, and is an excellent source of vitamins A and D. Shellfish is different again, as most of the varieties are encased in some sort of shell or body and although low in calories tends to be rather expensive.

All fish is delicate and should be treated with care. Never overcook or it will become dry and sometimes almost unpalatable; but it can be cooked in a variety of ways to suit your tastes – poaching, frying, grilling, baking, barbecuing.

Fish should always be used fresh, preferably on the day of purchase or within 24 hours, as it is highly perishable. The fish should smell fresh, have a bright eye and firm flesh. Flabby, stale looking or strong smelling fish is definitely old. Frozen fish should be thawed and then cooked quickly. Some fish products can be cooked from frozen and this together with the method will always be stated on the packet.

Fresh fish may be frozen after buying but never refreeze fish which has orginally been frozen – check with the fishmonger. Once the fish has been cooked it may then be frozen safely for up to one month regardless of whether the fish used was fresh or frozen. White fish will freeze for up to 9 months but oily fish is better used within 4–6 months. Shell fish freezes for up to 4 months.

Cider Soused Herrings

A family favourite with many but unknown to others. Traditionally served cold, it is however very good served hot with boiled or creamed potatoes.

Serves 4

300 ml (½ pint) dry cider
2 tablespoons vinegar
2 bay leaves
8 black peppercorns
pinch of ground allspice

salt and pepper
4 herrings, boned
2 onions, peeled and thinly sliced
chopped parsley to garnish

Preparation time: 20 minutes
Cooking time: 25 minutes
Heat the oven to 180°C/350°F/Gas mark 4.

Put the cider, vinegar, bay leaves, peppercorns, allspice and seasonings into a pan and bring to the boil. Loosely roll the herrings from head to tail, securing with a wooden cocktail stick if necessary, and place in a shallow ovenproof dish. Sprinkle the onion slices overall. Pour the liquid over the fish and cover with a lid or foil. Cook in a moderate oven for 20–25 minutes. Allow to cool, then chill thoroughly, and preferably leave for 24 hours to marinate before eating. Serve sprinkled with chopped parsley and crusty bread and butter.

Note: your fishmonger will usually bone the fish for you if you ask. If not it is quite easy to do yourself. Place the fish on a board and cut open from head to tail along the belly. Place with the inside of the fish on the board and lay it out so the silvery skin is upwards. Press firmly with your thumb along the backbone from head to tail several times until you feel the bones loosening. Turn the fish over and gently ease out the backbone and all the small bones with it.

Old Fashioned Kedgeree

Always a favourite and good to serve at any time of day.

Serves 4

225 g (8 oz) long grain rice
salt and black pepper

1 large onion, peeled and thinly sliced
50 g (2 oz) butter or margarine

1 clove garlic, crushed (optional)
350 g (12 oz) smoked haddock fillet
2 hard–boiled eggs, roughly chopped

2 tablespoons freshly chopped parsley
4–6 tablespoons single cream or yogurt

Preparation time: 20 minutes
Cooking time: 30 minutes

Cook the rice in boiling salted water until tender – about 13 minutes. Drain, rinse, then drain again thoroughly. Fry the onion very gently in the melted fat (adding garlic, if liked) for about 10 minutes until soft. Poach the haddock in the minimum of water until tender. Drain and flake, discarding any skin or bones. Add the fish, eggs, half the parsley, plenty of black pepper and the cream to the onions and heat through gently; then add the rice and heat again. Serve piping hot, sprinkled with the rest of the parsley.

Variations: for a real treat substitute part or all of the haddock with smoked salmon pieces or trimmings, or use all fresh salmon.

Cod à la Grecque

Fish makes a good quick casserole. Here it is flavoured with mushrooms, tomatoes, wine and garlic.

Serves 4

4 cod steaks
salt and pepper
1 tablespoon vegetable oil
1 onion, peeled and finely chopped
1 clove garlic, crushed
1 bay leaf
150 ml (¼ pint) dry white wine or cider

175 g (6 oz) button mushrooms,
  trimmed
2–3 tomatoes peeled, deseeded and cut
  into strips
chopped fresh mixed herbs or parsley to
  garnish

Preparation time: 15–20 minutes
Cooking time: 40 minutes
Heat the oven to 180°C/350°F/Gas mark 4.

Put the cod steaks into a fairly shallow lightly greased ovenproof dish or casserole and season lightly with salt and pepper. Heat the oil in a pan and fry the onion and garlic gently until soft but not coloured. Add the bay leaf, wine or cider and bring to the boil. If the mushrooms are large either cut into halves or quarters; otherwise leave whole and add to the sauce. Season lightly and spoon over the fish. Cover the dish with foil or a lid and cook in a moderate oven for 35–40 minutes or until the fish is tender. Add the tomato strips and return to the oven for a few minutes. Discard bay leaf and serve sprinkled liberally with freshly chopped herbs.

Freezing recommended: *for up to 1 month*

Mackerel Rolls With Orange Cider Sauce

Fresh mackerel is one of the best fishes around for flavour and with an orange and apple stuffing it is even better.

Serves 4

4 *small mackerel, cleaned and boned*
Stuffing:
1 small onion, peeled and finely chopped
50 g (2 oz) fresh breadcrumbs
1 level teaspoon grated orange rind
1 dessert apple, peeled, cored and grated
1 teaspoon lemon juice
salt and pepper
1 level tablespoon finely chopped
  parsley
2 tablespoons orange juice

Sauce:
2 egg yolks
2 tablespoons double cream
4 tablespoons dry cider
grated rind and juice of ½ orange
1 tablespoon lemon juice
pinch of cayenne pepper
25 g (1 oz) butter or margarine

To garnish:
orange slices
watercress

Preparation time: *25 minutes*
Cooking time: *40 minutes*
Heat the oven to 180°C/350°F/Gas mark 4.

Lay the fish out skinside downwards and remove any protruding bones. *For the stuffing:* combine all the ingredients except the orange juice, and dividing evenly between the fish, spread it smoothly over them. Roll up from head to tail and secure with wooden cocktail sticks. Place in a lightly greased ovenproof dish and pour the orange juice over them. Cover and cook in a moderate oven for 30–40 minutes until cooked through. *For the sauce:* beat together the egg yolks, cream, cider, orange rind and juice and lemon juice in a heatproof bowl. Stand over a pan of gently simmering water and heat gently, stirring continuously until the sauce is the consistency of pouring cream. Season, remove from the heat and beat in the butter. Serve the fish with the sauce spooned over them and garnish with orange and watercress.

Freezing recommended: *for up to 1 month*

Haddock Pulao

A rice dish flavoured with herbs, spices and fruit based on an Indian recipe, with haddock as the main ingredient.

Serves 4–6

1 onion, peeled and sliced
1–2 cloves garlic, crushed
2 tablespoons oil
450 g (1 lb) haddock fillets
600 ml (1 pint) stock or water
1 level teaspoon mixed herbs
1 level teaspoon whole coriander
6 black peppercorns
½ level teaspoon salt

1 jar mussels, in brine drained and/or
   100 g (4 oz) peeled prawns
225 g (8 oz) long grained rice
50 g (2 oz) walnut pieces or flaked
   almonds
2 dessert apples, cored and thickly sliced
40 g (1½ oz) raisins or sultanas
1 red pepper, deseeded and sliced
parsley and lemon wedges to garnish

Preparation time: *20 minutes*
Cooking time: *30 minutes*

Fry the onion and garlic gently in the oil until soft. Cut the fish into 5 cm (2 inch) pieces and add to the pan. Toss in the oil and then add the stock or water and bring to the boil. Add the herbs and spices, salt, mussels and/or prawns, rice, nuts, apples, raisins and red pepper. Cover the pan and simmer very gently for about 30 minutes or until the liquid is absorbed or the rice just cooked. Mix the fruit and vegetables gently into the rice and turn the mixture so the fish sits in a layer on the savoury rice. Garnish with lemon wedges and parsley.

Freezing recommended: *for up to 1 month*

Goujons of Plaice

These strips of plaice coated in egg and crumbs and fried are also good served cold, or as a cocktail party snack. The sauce can be varied – try a lightly curried mayonnaise, tartare or tomato sauce in place of hollandaise.

Serves 4

6–8 fillets of plaice (or lemon sole)
little seasoned flour
1–2 eggs, beaten
approx. 175 g (6 oz) freshly made fine
   white breadcrumbs or golden breadcrumbs
deep oil or fat for frying

Hollandaise sauce:
4 tablespoons wine or tarragon vinegar

4 peppercorns
2 tablespoons water
4 egg yolks
170 g (6 oz) butter, softened
little lemon juice
salt and pepper

To garnish:
cucumber slices
wedges of lemon

Preparation time: *30 minutes*
Cooking time: *15–30 minutes*

Cut the fillets into narrow strips about 1 cm (½ inch) thick across the fillets. Toss first in seasoned flour then dip in beaten egg and coat evenly and thoroughly in breadcrumbs. Chill for at least 10 minutes and preferably longer. Heat the deep fat until a cube of bread browns in about 30 seconds and fry the goujons a few at a time, until golden brown and cooked through –about 5 minutes. Alternatively they may be baked in a well greased baking tin in a single layer in a moderately hot oven (190°C/375°F/Gas Mark 5) for about 30 minutes or until browned and crispy. Drain on absorbent kitchen paper and keep warm.

While the goujons are cooking make the sauce: boil the vinegar with the peppercorns and water until reduced by half. Strain into a bowl and stand over a pan of gently simmering water. Beat in the egg yolks and cook very gently, stirring continuously until thickened – take care it does not scramble. Remove from the heat and beat in the butter, a knob at a time, until incorporated and the sauce reaches the desired consistency. Sharpen with lemon juice and adjust the seasoning. Serve with the goujons which should be garnished with the cucumber slices and lemon.

Freezing recommended: *for up to 1 month*

Seafish Pie

A basic fish pie with interesting additions.

Serves 4

450 g (1 lb) white fish fillets (cod, haddock, whiting, plaice etc.)
juice of ½ lemon
1 bay leaf
salt and pepper
300 ml (½ pint) milk or milk and water mixed
65 g (2½ oz) butter or margarine
1 onion, peeled and thinly sliced
1 clove garlic, crushed
25 g (1 oz) flour
4 tablespoons dry white wine or cider

1 level teaspoon dried basil or 1 level teaspoon freshly chopped basil
50 g–150 g (2–4 oz) peeled prawns
1 jar mussels, drained or 2 hard-boiled eggs, roughly chopped
1 level tablespoon capers
675 g–900 g (1½ –2 lbs) potatoes, peeled and boiled
2–4 tablespoons top of the milk

To garnish:
few whole prawns
fresh basil or parsley sprigs

Preparation time: *25 minutes,*
Cooking time: *30 minutes*
Heat the oven to 200°C/400°F/Gas Mark 6.

Put the fresh fish into a pan with the lemon juice, bay leaf, seasonings and milk. Bring to the boil, and simmer for 12–15 minutes until tender. Drain off the liquor and reserve. Flake the fish, remove any skin and bones. Melt

400 g (1½ oz) butter in a pan and fry the onion and garlic gently until soft. Stir in the flour and cook for a minute or so, then add the wine or cider and 250 ml (8 fl oz) of the cooking liquor. Bring to the boil, add the basil and simmer for 2–3 minutes. Adjust the seasonings and stir in the white fish, prawns, mussels or eggs and capers and turn into a fairly shallow oven-proof dish. Sieve the potato and beat in the remaining butter and milk. Put into a piping bag fitted with a star vegetable nozzle and pipe a row or two of potato around the edge of the dish, leaving the centre uncovered. Cook in a fairly hot oven for about 30 minutes or until the potato begins to brown. Garnish with prawns and herbs.

Freezing recommended: *for up to 1 month.*

Trout with Watercress and Lemon Stuffing

Rainbow or pink trout can be used for this recipe, or if preferred, herrings or small mackerel.

Serves 4

4 trout
1 bunch watercress
25 g (1 oz) butter or margarine
1 small onion, peeled and finely chopped
grated rind of 1 lemon
2 teaspoons lemon juice
75 g (3 oz) fresh white breadcrumbs
¼ level teaspoon ground coriander
salt and pepper

300 ml (½ pint) fish stock (see page 13)
   or 150 ml (¼ pint) each white wine
   and water
4 tablespoons cream

To garnish:
lemon slices
watercress

Preparation time: *25–30 minutes*
Cooking time: *30 minutes*
Heat the oven to 190°C/375°F/Gas Mark 5.

Bone the fish but leave the heads and tails on (you can ask the fishmonger to do this for you if you prefer). If you want to make fish stock use the bones as on page 13. *For the stuffing:* reserve a few pieces of watercress for garnish and chop the remainder. Melt the fat in a pan and fry the onions until soft. Turn into a bowl and add the lemon rind, juice, breadcrumbs, coriander, season-ings and chopped watercress. Mix well and use to stuff the fish. Lay them in a fairly shallow ovenproof dish and season well. Pour the hot stock or wine and water round the fish and cover with foil. Cook in a moderately hot oven for 25–30 minutes until tender. Drain the cooking liquor into a heavy–based saucepan and boil hard until reduced by about half. Add the cream and reheat gently. Adjust seasonings and serve the fish with a little sauce spooned over each one. Garnish with lemon and watercress.

Freezing recommended: *for up to 1 month*

Sweet and Sour Halibut Steaks

For a more economical dish you can use cod steaks or cutlets in place of halibut.

Serves 4

4 halibut steaks
4 tablespoons medium sherry
1 tablespoon lemon juice
6 tablespoons orange juice
  (unsweetened)
3 tablespoons light soy sauce
2 level tablespoons demerara sugar
salt and pepper

grated rind of ½ orange
225 g (8 oz) can water chestnuts,
  drained and sliced

To garnish:
Spring onion tassels
watercress
orange slices

Preparation time: *15 minutes, plus standing time*
Cooking time: *20 minutes*

Place the halibut in a single layer in a shallow dish. Combine the sherry, lemon juice, 4 tablespoons orange juice, soy sauce, sugar and a pinch of salt and pepper. Pour over the fish, cover and leave to marinate in a cool place for 1–2 hours, turning over once. Place the drained fish in a foil–lined grill pan and cook under a moderate grill for 7–8 minutes each side, until just cooked through. Keep warm. Meanwhile transfer the marinade, remaining orange juice and rind to a small saucepan and bring to the boil. Add the sliced water chestnuts and simmer for 3–4 minutes until the sauce begins to turn slightly syrupy. Adjust seasonings and serve each steak with the sauce spooned over and garnished with spring onion tassels, watercress and orange slices.

Freezing recommended: *for up to 1 month*

Spring Onion Tassels – Trim spring onions so they are about 6 cm (2½ inches) long; then cut off the roots. Using either a pair of scissors or a sharp knife cut into the top of the onion to within 2 cm (¾ inch) of the base as many times as possible cutting it into strips. Put into iced water and chill for several hours so it opens up and curls. Drain well before use.

Special Fish Pie

White fish poached in cider and flavoured with dill and red pimientos form the base of this fish pie.

Serves 4

450 g (1 lb) cod or haddock fillet,
  skinned
300 ml (½ pint) medium cider

salt and pepper
little milk
2 canned red pimientos, cut into strips

1 level tablespoon fresh dill, chopped or
  1–2 level teaspoons dried dillweed
2 hard–boiled eggs, sliced
50 g (2 oz) butter or margarine

100 g (4 oz) mushrooms, sliced
40 g (1½ oz) flour
675 g (1½ lb) cooked, mashed potatoes
25 g (1 oz) Cheddar cheese, grated

Preparation time: 25 minutes
Cooking time: 30 minutes
Heat the oven to 200°C/400°F/Gas Mark 6.

Poach the fish in the cider with the seasonings for about 10 minutes or until just tender. Lift out the fish, measure the poaching liquor and make up to 400 ml (scant ¾ pint) with milk. Flake the fish and mix with the pimiento, dill and eggs. Melt the fat in a pan, add the mushrooms and cook for a minute or two; stir in the flour and cook for a minute longer. Gradually add the fish liquor and bring to the boil, stirring continuously. Simmer for 2 minutes then season well and combine with the fish mixture. Turn into an ovenproof dish and pipe or spread the potato round the edges of the dish. Sprinkle the uncovered filling with cheese and cook in a fairly hot oven for 30 minutes or until lightly browned on top. Serve hot.

Freezing recommended: for up to 1 month

Crab au Gratin

Crabmeat is readily available in frozen form as well as canned and is also often found in fish shops and supermarkets fresh and ready dressed.

Serves 2

25 g (1 oz) butter or margarine
1 small onion, peeled and finely chopped
25 g (1 oz) flour
250 ml (8 fl oz) milk
salt and black pepper
¼ level teaspoon dry mustard
2 teaspoons lemon juice
50 g (2 oz) mushrooms, chopped

225 g (8 oz) crabmeat (from one dressed
  crab or canned or frozen)
25 g (1 oz) fresh breadcrumbs
25 g (1 oz) mature Cheddar cheese,
  finely grated

To garnish:
parsley sprigs
lemon wedges

Preparation time: 20 minutes
Cooking time: 10 minutes

Melt the butter in a pan and fry the onion gently until soft, but not coloured. Stir in the flour and cook for a minute or so then gradually add the milk and bring to the boil, stirring frequently. Season well with salt and pepper and add the mustard, lemon juice and mushrooms; simmer for 2–3 minutes. Stir in the crabmeat and cook for a further two minutes or until piping hot; adjust the seasonings. Spoon into one large or two individual flameproof dishes. Combine the breadcrumbs and cheese and sprinkle over the crab. Cook under a moderate grill until the topping is well browned. Garnish with parsley and lemon.

Note: the filling can also be used to fill 4–6 avocado halves and then brown under the grill or bake in the oven at 180°C/350°F/Gas Mark 4 for about 20 minutes.

Salmon Mousse

Everyone's favourite, this time set in a ring mould and garnished with smoked salmon and cucumber.

Serves 6–8

25 g (1 oz) butter or margarine
25 g (1 oz) flour
300 ml (½ pint) milk
½ level teaspoon made mustard
salt and pepper
1 tablespoon white wine vinegar
3 eggs (size 2 or 3), separated
300–350 g (10–12 oz) cooked (or
  canned) salmon, flaked

150 ml (¼ pint) double cream
4 level teaspoons powdered gelatine

To garnish:
50 g (2 oz) smoked salmon
chopped cucumber
stuffed green olives
frisée or curly endive

Preparation time: *30 minutes*

Melt the butter in a pan, stir in the flour and cook for a minute or so. Gradually add the milk and bring to the boil, stirring continuously. Add the mustard, seasonings and vinegar and simmer for 2 minutes. Beat in the egg yolks and continue to simmer for another minute. Remove from the heat and then beat in the flaked salmon and cream. Dissolve the gelatine in 2 tablespoons water in a small basin over a pan of simmering water or in the microwave set on medium for a minute or so; then stir evenly through the mousse and leave until on the point of setting. Whip the egg whites stiffly and fold through the mousse. Quickly pour into a greased 1 litre (1½ pint) ring mould, fish mould or other mould and chill until set.

To serve turn out the mould carefully and if using a ring mould, fill the centre with frisée; for other moulds or shapes arrange frisée and chopped cucumber around the mould and finish with small rolls of smoked salmon and stuffed olives.

Freezing recommended: *for up to 1 month*

Salmon en Croûte

A very elegant dish fit for any smart dinner party or just for serving to friends.

Serves 6–8

1.5 kg (3–3½ lb) fresh salmon, cleaned
  and head removed
juice of 1 lemon
salt and pepper
50 g (2 oz) butter, softened

2 teaspoons freshly chopped dillweed
  or 1 level teaspoon dried dillweed
450 g (1 lb) puff pastry
beaten egg to glaze

Preparation time: 45–60 minutes
Cooking time: 50 minutes
Heat the oven to 200°C/400°F/Gas Mark 6.

Ask the fishmonger to fillet the fish for you. Alternatively, take a sharp filleting knife and cut along the backbone beginning at the head and working to the tail and at the same time running the knife blade at an angle to the bone. With a slicing movement the flesh will ease from the bone. Continue to cut, keeping in line with the backbone until the fillet becomes free; then work the other side of the bone until the fillet is just attached by the tail. Cut this off, then turn the fish over and do the same to the other side. Next remove the skin from the fillets: place the fillet on a board skinside downwards, raise the flesh slightly at the tail and hold the tail firmly. Run the knife blade towards the head of the fish pressing it firmly to the surface so all the flesh is removed from the skin. Discard skin or use with the bones and head to make fish stock.

Rub the fillets all over with lemon juice and season lightly with salt and pepper. Lay one fillet on a board and spread with the butter, then sprinkle with the dill and cover with the second fillet to reshape the fish. Roll out about three–quarters of the pastry very thinly and use to enclose the fish, keeping to the shape as much as possible and sealing the edges with beaten egg. Roll out the reserved pastry with the trimmings and use to cut into 'scales'. Arrange these scales all over the fish working from head to tail. Cut out a pastry tail and an eye for the head. Position these and glaze completely.

Cook in a fairly hot oven for 30 minutes then reduce to moderately hot (190°C/375°F/Gas Mark 5) and continue cooking for a further 20 minutes. When sufficiently browned, lay a sheet of greaseproof paper lightly over the pastry. Serve the salmon hot or cold garnished with lemon, cucumber and fresh dill and with Hollandaise sauce.

Freezing recommended: for up to 1 month

MEAT AND POULTRY

INTRODUCTION

For many people meat is one of the most important, satisfying and versatile of foods. There are, of course, others who disagree. There are also a number of people who have a preference for white meats in the form of chicken and turkey and possibly other poultry, and they tend to use only recipes for white meats, only turning occasionally to red meat.

However, for the large proportion of people who do eat all types of meat and poultry, these foods do supply a tremendous amount of protein and some of the B vitamins and are a good source of iron. The fat on meat provides energy and brings out much of the flavour. It also helps the meat to keep moist during cooking; but of course poultry, particularly chicken and turkey, has virtually no fat and is very low in calories, making it very popular with weight-watchers.

As a general rule when selecting meat it should have a certain amount of fat on it, but not an excessive amount and this fat should be firm and free from any discolouration. Likewise, poultry should have firm flesh with no stale or strong smell and the skin should be unblemished. It is essential, particularly when buying any type of frozen poultry and game, to ensure that it is completely thawed before cooking. Those lurking ice crystals in the cavity of poultry will slow down the cooking enormously and often produce a bird that is not properly cooked which could lead to food poisoning.

Many of the recipes included here can satisfactorily be frozen once cooked but it is better to thaw them completely before re–cooking and on no account should they just be 'warmed through', they must be re–cooked. It is quite safe to freeze cooked dishes that have been made with previously frozen meat or poultry and most will store satisfactorily in the freezer for up to 6–8 weeks. Those highly flavoured with onions and spices are best used within a month.

Do not take short cuts when it comes to cooking meat, it does need the times suggested in the recipes to ensure tenderness and succulence; increasing the oven temperature and cutting the cooking time does not work.

Some of the dishes can be adapted to cooking in the microwave, but refer to the microwave handbook for suggested cooking time. Re–cooking and particularly re–heating a plate of food for someone coming home late are excellent in the microwave. Cover and cook a plate full for about 2 minutes on High/100%; check and if not hot enough continue for another ½–1 minute.

ROASTING CHARTS

Beef
Meat on the bone

	Moderately hot 190°C/375°F/ Gas Mark 5	*Hot* 220°C/425°F/ Gas Mark 7
Rare	20 mins per 450g (1 lb) plus 20 mins	15 mins per 450 g (1 lb) plus 15 mins
Medium	25 mins per 450g (1 lb) plus 25 mins	20 mins per 450 g (1 lb) plus 20 mins
Well done	30–35 mins per 450g (1 lb) plus 30 mins	25–30 mins per 450g (1 lb) plus 25 mins

Meat boned and rolled

Rare	25 mins per 450g (1 lb) plus 25 mins	20 mins per 450 g (1 lb) plus 20 mins
Medium	30 mins per 450g (1 lb) plus 30 mins	25 mins per 450g (1 lb) plus 25 mins
Well done	35–40 mins per 450g (1 lb) plus 35 mins	30–35 mins per 450g (1 lb) plus 30 mins

Lamb

	Moderately hot 180°C/350°F/ Gas Mark 4	*Hot* 220°C/425°F/ Gas Mark 7
Meat on the bone	30–35 mins per 450 g (1 lb) depending on thickness of the joint	20 mins per 450 g (1 lb) plus 20 mins
Meat boned and rolled	40–45 mins per 450 g (1 lb) depending on thickness of joint	25 mins per 450 g (1 lb) plus 25 mins

Pork

	Moderately hot 190°C/375°F/ Gas Mark 5	*Hot* 220°C/425°F/ Gas Mark 7

Pork on the bone

25–30 mins per 450 g
(1 lb) plus 25 mins

Pork boned and rolled

30–35 mins per 450g
(1 lb) plus 30 mins

Turkey

In a moderate oven at 180°C/350°F/Gas Mark 4

Weight	Without Foil	With foil
2.25–3.5kg (5–8 lb)	2–2½ hours	2½–3½ hours
3.5–5kg (8–11 lb)	2½–3½ hours	3½–4 hours
5–6.75kg (11–15 lb)	3¼–3¾ hours	4–5 hours
6.75–9kg (15–20 lb)	3¾–4¼ hours	5–5½ hours

Goose

Moderately hot
180°C/350°F/Gas Mark 4
25–30 mins per 450 g
(1 lb)

Hot
200°C/400°F/Gas Mark 6
15 mins per 450 g
(1 lb) plus 15 mins over

Duck

Fairly hot to hot oven
200–225°C/400–425°F/Gas Mark 6–7
20 mins per 450g (1 lb)

Chicken

Fairly hot oven
200°C/400°F/Gas Mark 6
20 mins per 450g (1 lb) plus 20 mins

Spicy Brisket Pot Roast

Brisket is one of the cheapest yet tastiest cuts of beef. Make sure you cook a large enough piece for it is excellent served cold.

Serves 6–8

1.8 kg (4 lb) lean brisket joint of beef,
*   boned and rolled*
150 ml (¼ pint) red wine
2 tablespoons oil or dripping
150 ml (¼ pint) beef stock
salt and pepper
small stick of cinnamon
10 whole cloves

6 onions, peeled and halved
450 g (1 lb) carrots, peeled
6 sticks celery, scrubbed and thickly
*   sliced*
450 g (1 lb) potatoes, peeled and cut
*   into large cubes*
1 level tablespoon cornflour (optional)

Preparation time: *20 minutes plus marinating time*
Cooking time: *3½ – 4 hours*
Heat the oven to 160°C/325°F/Gas Mark 3.

Place the beef in a large dish or large thick polythene bag and pour the wine over it. Cover and leave to marinate in a cool place for at least 12 hours, turning it several times. Remove the meat and pat dry. Fry in heated oil until well browned all over then place in a large deep ovenproof dish. Add the stock and seasonings to the wine marinade, bring to the boil, pour over the beef and add the cinnamon stick and cloves. Cover tightly and cook in a very moderate oven for 1½ hours. Add the onions, carrots, celery and potatoes and cover tightly again. Return to the oven for another 2–2½ hours or until tender.

Remove the joint and place on a serving dish; drain the vegetables and place around the joint or in a separate bowl, keep warm. Meanwhile skim the fat from the juices in the casserole. If liked, thicken with the cornflour blended in a little cold water. Bring back to the boil, adjust the seasonings, and serve the sauce separately, but with the beef and vegetables.

Devilled Meatballs

A quick, economical casserole to serve at any time.

Serves 4–5

550 g (1¼ lb) raw minced beef
40 g (1½ oz) fresh breadcrumbs, brown
  or white
1 small onion, peeled and finely chopped
salt and pepper
1 tablespoon Worcestershire sauce
2 tablespoons oil

Sauce:
1 level tablespoon flour

1½ level teaspoons dry mustard
1½ level teaspoons Dijon mustard
1 tablespoon soy sauce
1 tablespoon Worcestershire sauce
300 ml (½ pint) beef stock
225 g (8 oz) carrots, peeled and cut into
  thin sticks
1 large cooking apple, peeled, cored and
  diced
watercress or parsley to garnish

Preparation time: 25 minutes
Cooking time: 45 minutes
Heat the oven to 180°C/350°F/Gas Mark 4.

Mix together the minced beef, breadcrumbs, onion, a little salt and pepper and the Worcestershire sauce. Divide into 16 and shape into neat balls. Heat the oil in a pan and fry the meatballs until browned all over. Place in a casserole. Pour off all but 1 tablespoon fat from the pan and stir in the flour and dry mustard. Cook for 1 minute, stirring continuously. Add the Dijon mustard, soy sauce and Worcestershire sauces and the stock and bring to the boil. Season to taste, simmer for a minute or so then add the carrots and apple to the sauce. Pour over the meatballs, mix gently and cover the casserole. Cook in a moderate oven for about 45 minutes. Remove the lid from the casserole and spoon off any fat from the surface. Serve garnished with watercress or parsley and with spaghetti, noodles or creamed potatoes.

Freezing recommended: for up to 2 months. Thaw completely before re–cooking.

Mairangi Beef

A rich beef casserole flavoured with wine, tomatoes and capers ideal for a dinner party or everyday eating.

Serves 6

900 g (2 lb) braising steak
salt and pepper
2 tablespoons oil
2 large onions, peeled and sliced
1 clove garlic, crushed
2 level tablespoons flour
150 ml (¼ pint) red wine

150 ml (¼ pint) beef stock
425 g (15 oz) can tomatoes
1 level tablespoon tomato purée
2 level tablespoons capers
1 tablespoon wine vinegar
parsley to garnish

Preparation time: *20 minutes*
Cooking time: *2½ hours*
Heat the oven to 160°C/325°F/Gas Mark 3.

Cut the meat into 12 even–sized pieces, trimming off any excess fat or gristle. Season lightly with salt and pepper. Heat the oil in a pan and fry the meat until well sealed all over then transfer to a casserole. Fry the onions and garlic gently in the same fat until soft and lightly browned. Stir in the flour and cook for a minute or so, stirring frequently. Add the wine, stock, tomatoes, tomato purée, capers and vinegar and bring to the boil. Simmer for a minute or so and season lightly. Pour over the meat, cover the casserole tightly and cook in a moderate oven for 2½ hours or until tender. Adjust the seasonings and serve with new potatoes tossed in chopped parsley or with baked jacket potatoes and a green vegetable.

Freezing recommended: *for up to 2 months. Thaw completely before re–cooking.*

Perryland Steak

Steaks cooked with a mixture of pepper, mushrooms, wine, mustard and garlic.

Serves 4

4 quick fry or entrecote steaks
salt and pepper
1 clove garlic, crushed
25 g (1 oz) butter or margarine
1 tablespoon oil
1 onion, peeled and thinly sliced
1 small red pepper, deseeded and sliced

100 g (4 oz) button mushrooms, quar-
tered
4 tablespoons wine, red or white
1 teaspoon Worcestershire sauce
1½ level tablespoons coarse grained
mustard

Preparation time: *15 minutes*
Cooking time: *15 minutes*

Trim the steaks, season lightly and rub with crushed garlic. Heat the fat and oil in a pan and add the onion and pepper. Cook gently until soft, add the mushrooms and continue for a minute or so. Push the vegetables to the side of the pan and add the steaks. Cook quickly to seal on both sides then lower the heat and spread the vegetables over the steaks. Blend the wine, Worcestershire sauce and mustard together and add to the pan. Simmer for 2–3 minutes turning the steaks once. Adjust the seasonings and serve from the pan.

Barlavington Hotpot

A good beefy hotpot flavoured with brown ale, prunes and apricot.

Serves 4–5

675 g (1½ lb) stewing or braising beef,
   cut into 2.5 cm/1 inch cubes
3 tablespoons oil
2 onions, peeled and sliced
25 g (1 oz) flour
300 ml (½ pint) brown ale
250 g (8 fl oz) beef stock
1½ level teaspoons tomato purée

½ level teaspoon mixed herbs (optional)
100 g (4 oz) no–need–to–soak prunes
50–100 g (2–4 oz) no–need–to–soak
  apricots, halved
salt and pepper
675 g (1½) potatoes, peeled and sliced
15 g (½ oz) butter, melted
chopped parsley to garnish

Preparation time: *25 minutes*
Cooking time: *2½ hours*
Heat the oven to 180°C/350°F/Gas Mark 4.

Brown the beef all over in the oil and transfer to a casserole. Fry the onions in the fat until soft. Spoon off the excess fat from the pan, then stir the flour into the remaining juices and cook for a minute or so. Add the ale, stock, tomato purée and herbs (if used) and bring to the boil. Add the prunes, apricot and seasonings to taste and simmer for 2–3 minutes. Pour over the beef and mix well. Arrange slices of potato evenly over the contents of the casserole and brush the top with melted butter. Cover with foil and cook in a moderate oven for 2 hours. Remove the foil and either increase the oven temperature to hot (220°C/425°F/Gas Mark 7) and cook for a further 20 minutes until the potatoes have browned; or place under a moderate grill to brown.

Freezing recommended: *for up to 2 months. Thaw completely before re–cooking.*

Top: *Fish Terrine with Smoked Salmon, Duck Terrine, Cheese and Walnut Pâté.*
Bottom: *Trout with Watercress and Lemon Stuffing, Seafish Pie, Sweet and Sour Halibut Steaks.*

Above: Leek, Bacon and Pineapple Salad, Leek and Onion Tartlets.
Left: Avocado and Egg Salad, Minted Melon Salad, Rosy Red Chicken Salad.

Roast Turkey

Catalina Pork

Top left: Coffee Syllabubs, Coffee Walnut Meringues, Coffee Malakoff Cake, Crêpes Suzette.
Bottom left: Courgette and Tarragon Quiches, Pinwheel Sandwiches, Sausage and Salami Rolls, Orange and Cardamom Biscuits, Cranberry Teabread, Lime Creams, Hazelnut Florentines.
Above: Apple Strudel.

Avocado and Crab Cocktails, Duck·with Orange and Cranberry Sauce, Red Cabbage and Leek Medley, Mixed Salad with Fennel and Watercress, Brown Rice and Peanut Salad, Chocolate Blackcurrant Gâteau, Peach and Banana Syllabubs.

Lamb Quickie Grills

For anyone in a hurry lamb chops are always a good idea, but with one of the following toppings they are just as quick and twice as tasty.

1–2 lamb chops per person (e.g. butter-fly or double loin, loin, chump or cutlets)
salt and pepper

1 tablespoon per person of one of the fol-lowing:–
mint jelly, cranberry jelly, ginger pre-serve, coarse orange marmalade
watercress and tomatoes to garnish

Preparation time: *5 minutes*
Cooking time: *10 minutes*

Trim the chops if necessary and season well. A little garlic may be added, if liked. Place the chops in a foil lined grill pan and cook under a moderate heat for about 5 minutes. Turn over and cook for a further 2–3 minutes. Spread with the chosen topping and continue cooking for about 5 minutes or until cooked through and the chops are well browned with a bubbling topping. Serve hot garnished with tomatoes (either halved and grilled or raw in slices) and sprigs of watercress.

Roast Lamb with Cashew Nut Stuffing ·

This stuffing can also be used with other meats and poultry.

Serves 5–6

1.5–1.75 kg (3½–4 lb) double loin of lamb joint, boned
salt and pepper
6–8 potatoes, peeled and halved
little oil or dripping

Stuffing:
1 onion, peeled and chopped
25 g (1 oz) butter or margarine
100 g (4 oz) mushrooms, chopped

1 level tablespoon freshly chopped parsley
1 level teaspoon dried thyme
50 g (2 oz) cashew nuts, chopped
75 g (3 oz) fresh white breadcrumbs
1 egg, beaten

To garnish:
1 kiwi fruit, sliced
450 g (1 lb) carrots, cooked
parsley sprigs

Preparation time: *20 minutes*
Cooking time: *2–2½ hours*
Heat the oven to 200°C/400°F/Gas Mark 6.

Open out the lamb and season the inside lightly. *For the stuffing:* fry the onion gently in the fat until soft. Add the mushrooms and continue frying for a minute or so. Remove from the heat, stir in the parsley, thyme, nuts and seasonings. Add the breadcrumbs and sufficient egg to bind together. Spread the stuffing over the inside of the lamb. Roll and secure with skewers and/or string. Stand in a roasting tin and surround with peeled potatoes. Pour 3–4 tablespoons oil over the joint or spread with a little drip-ping and season well. Roast in a fairly hot oven allowing 30 minutes per 450 g (1 lb) and 20 minutes extra. Baste several time during cooking and turn the potatoes over half–way through cooking. Garnish with slices of carrot and arrange kiwi fruit slices down the centre of the joint. Serve the potatoes separately and garnish overall with parsley.

Freezing recommended: *for up to 2 months*

Note: This joint is also good served cold in slices with salad.

Apricot Lamb en Croûte

Boned leg of lamb with a stuffing based on sausagemeat and apricots and baked in a puff pastry case to serve hot or cold.

Serves 8–10

1 leg of lamb (approx 2.25 kg/5 lb)
225 g (8 oz) pork sausagemeat
50 g (2oz) fresh breadcrumbs
4 rashers streaky bacon, derinded and
  chopped
1 onion, peeled and finely chopped
1 clove garlic, crushed
200 g (7 oz) can apricots, drained and
  chopped

salt and black pepper
2 level tablespoons freshly chopped
  parsley
1 level teaspoon freshly chopped mint or
  ½ level teaspoon dried mint
little oil
450 g (1 lb) puff pastry, thawed if
  frozen
beaten egg to glaze

Preparation time: *45 minutes*
Cooking time: *2¾ hours*
Heat the oven to 200°C/400°F/Gas Mark 4

Bone the leg of lamb (or ask your butcher to do it for you). Combine the sausagemeat, breadcrumbs, bacon, onion, garlic, apricots, seasonings and herbs and bind with a little apricot juice, if necessary. Use to stuff the lamb securing with wooden cocktail sticks or skewers. Place in a roasting tin with a little oil and plenty of seasonings. Cook in a fairly hot oven for 1½–2 hours, basting regularly until almost cooked.

Remove and cool as quickly as possible. Roll out the pastry on a floured surface. Stand the cold joint in the centre and wrap in the pastry, dampen-ing the edges with water to seal. Turn over carefully so the pastry join is underneath then place in a lightly greased roasting tin and glaze with beaten egg. Decorate with the pastry trimmings, glaze again and bake in a fairly hot oven for about 40 minutes or until well browned. Serve hot with vegetables or leave to cool and chill before serving in slices with salads.

Freezing recommended: *for up to 2 months. Thaw completely before re–cooking.*

Lamb Steaks Wairapa

Leg steaks of lamb are taken from the top of the leg and make an excellent meal.

Serves 4

4 lamb leg steaks
salt and pepper
25 g (1 oz) butter or margarine
2 tablespoons oil

Sauce:
25 g (1 oz) butter
1 onion, peeled and finely chopped
25 g (1 oz) flour
150 ml (¼ pint) milk

150 ml (¼ pint) soured cream
½–¾ cucumber
2 teaspoons freshly chopped fennel or
  dill or 1 level teaspoon dried dillweed
1 hard–boiled egg, coarsely grated or
  finely chopped
sprigs of fennel, dill or parsley to
  garnish

Preparation time: *20–25 minutes*
Cooking time: *15 minutes*

Place the steaks betwen 2 sheets of cling film or damp greaseproof paper and beat out each steak until even. Remove and season well. *For the sauce:* melt the butter in the pan and fry the onion until soft but not coloured. Stir in the flour and cook for 1 minute. Stir in the milk gradually and bring to the boil; simmer for a minute or so then stir in the soured cream and bring back to the boil, stirring continuously. Season well. Finely chop most of the cucumber and stir into the sauce with the fennel or dill and grated egg. Keep warm.

Heat the butter and oil in a frying pan and fry the lamb steaks for 4–5 minutes each side or until browned and cooked through – but take care not to overcook. Arrange the steaks on a serving dish and spoon the sauce across the centre. Garnish with the remaining cucumber cut into slices and with the fennel or parsley. Serve at once.

Somerset Pork

Pork and cider blend well together and although the recipe uses boneless pork slices, pork chops would do just as well.

Serves 4

4 boneless pork slices
2 level tablespoons seasoned flour
400 g (1½ oz) butter or margarine
175 g (6 oz) button mushrooms,
trimmed and halved

300 ml (½ pint) dry cider
1 teaspoon Worcestershire sauce
salt and pepper
150 ml (¼ pint) soured cream
parsley to garnish

Preparation time: *20 minutes*
Cooking time: *25 minutes*

Trim the pork and coat in seasoned flour. Fry in the melted butter until brown on both sides and almost cooked through. Remove from the pan and keep warm. Add mushrooms to the pan and cook gently for 2–3 minutes. Stir in any remaining flour and cook for a minute or so. Gradually add the cider and bring to the boil; add the Worcestershire sauce and season well. Replace the pork, cover and simmer gently for about 10 minutes. Stir cream until smooth then stir evenly through the sauce in the pan. Reheat, adjust the seasonings and serve garnished with parsley.

Freezing recommended: *for up to 2 months. Thaw completely before re–cooking.*

Catalina Pork

Flavoured with cumin and coriander this spicy dish is topped with herb and nut dumplings.

Serves 4

675 g (1½ lb) lean pork, cubed
2 tablespoons oil
1 large onion, peeled and sliced
2 cloves garlic, crushed
1 level tablespoon flour
450 ml (¾ pint) stock
2 level teaspoons ground cumin
2 level teaspoons ground coriander
salt and pepper
6 sticks celery, sliced
150–300 ml (¼–½ pint) thick set natural
yogurt

Parsley and Pecan Dumplings:
100 g (4 oz) self–raising flour
salt
50 g (2 oz) shredded suet
250 g (10 oz) shelled pecan nuts, chopped
2 level tablespoons freshly chopped parsley
2–3 tablespoons cold water

Preparation time: *25 minutes*
Cooking time: *1 hour*
Heat the oven to 180°C/350°F/Gas Mark 4.

Trim the pork if necessary and brown lightly in the oil. Transfer to a casserole. Fry the onion and garlic gently in the same fat until soft but not coloured. Stir in the flour and cook for a minute or so then add the stock, cumin and coriander and bring to the boil, stirring frequently. Season well and pour over the pork. Add the celery, mix well and cover. Cook in a moderate oven for about 40 minutes.

For the dumplings: sift the flour with a pinch of salt and mix in the suet, nuts and parsley. Add sufficient water to mix to a soft dough and shape into 8–12 balls. Stir 150 ml (¼ pint) yogurt into the casserole and place the dumplings on top. Replace the lid and return to the oven for 15–20 minutes until the dumplings are risen and light. Serve with green vegetables and potatoes, and if liked, an extra spoonful of yogurt on each portion.

Freezing recommended: *for up to 2 months. Thaw completely before re–cooking.*

Pork Satay with Yellow Rice

The pork can be marinated for up to 12 hours before cooking and the sauce made in advance. Chicken or turkey breast meat can be used as an alternative to pork.

Serves 4

550 g (1¼ lb) lean raw pork
4 teaspoons dry sherry
4 teaspoons soy sauce
4 teaspoons sesame oil (or other oil)
finely grated rind and juice of 1 small
    lemon
4 level teaspoons sesame seeds

Peanut Sauce:
150 ml (¼ pint) boiling water
50 g (2 oz) desiccated coconut
100 g (4oz) crunchy peanut butter

½ level teaspoon mild chilli powder
2 level teaspoons any brown sugar
2 teaspoons soy sauce
1 level teaspoon finely snipped chives or
    spring onion tops

Yellow Rice:
225 g (8 oz) long grain rice
1 level teaspoon turmeric
1 yellow pepper, finely chopped
paprika to garnish

Preparation time: *15 minutes, plus marinating time*
Cooking time: *20 minutes*

Cut the pork into 2.5 cm (1 inch) cubes. Combine the sherry, soy sauce, sesame oil, lemon rind and juice and sesame seeds, pour over the pork and mix well. Cover and chill for at least 3 hours and up to 12 hours. *For the sauce:* pour the boiling water over the coconut and leave until cold. Transfer into a saucepan and heat gently. Stir in the peanut butter until melted and then add the chilli powder, sugar, soy sauce and chives and mix until well-blended. Bring to the boil for a minute or so then turn into a bowl and leave until cold. When ready to cook, thread the pork onto 4 skewers and cook under a moderate grill for about 5–6 minutes each side, brushing again with the marinade when turning over. Serve with yellow rice and the sauce.

For the yellow rice: Cook the rice in plenty of boiling salted water with turmeric added. When almost tender add the yellow pepper and continue cooking for 2 minutes. Drain very well and serve lightly dusted with paprika.

Honey Baked Ham

Everyone likes a piece of ham, and when home cooked it always tastes even better.

Serves 8–10

1.8–2.2 kg (4–5 lbs) joint gammon or
    prime collar bacon, boned and rolled
6 tablespoons thick honey
whole cloves

425 g (15 oz) can pineapple rings

To garnish:
Chicory leaves
watercress

Preparation time: *20 minutes, plus soaking time*
Cooking time: *2–2½ hours*

Soak the joint overnight in cold water. Drain and place in a saucepan with fresh water. Calculate the cooking time allowing 25 minutes per 450 g (1lb) and 25 minutes over. Bring to the boil, cover and simmer for half the cooking time. Heat the oven to 180°C/350°F/Gas Mark 4. Drain joint and remove the rind. Score the fat into diamonds with a sharp knife and stand in a baking tin. Spread the honey over the fat, stud the diamonds with cloves and add 150 ml (¼ pint) of the pineapple juice to the tin. Roast in a moderate oven for the remainder of the cooking time, increasing the oven temperature to hot (220°C/435°F/Gas Mark 7) for the last 20 minutes. Baste the joint with the pineapple juice every 15 minutes during cooking. Serve hot or cold, garnished with pineapple rings, chicory leaves and watercress.

Polynesian Chicken

This chicken dish has a taste of the sunshine with pawpaws, pepper and spices.

Serves 6

6 chicken portions or boneless breast
portions
salt and pepper
paprika
40 g (1½ oz) butter or margarine
2 tablespoons oil
300 ml (½ pint) fresh orange juice

juice of 1 lime or lemon
2 teaspoons soy sauce
1 tablespoon clear honey
½ level teaspoon ground ginger
¼ level teaspoon garlic salt or powdered
garlic
1 pawpaw
1 green pepper, finely chopped

Preparation time: *25 minutes*
Cooking time: *50 minutes*
Heat the oven to 190°C/325°F/Gas Mark 3.

Season the chicken well with salt, pepper and paprika. Fry the chicken in a mixture of butter and oil and until well–browned all over; transfer to a shallow ovenproof casserole. Combine the orange and lime juice, soy sauce, honey, ginger, garlic and seasonings. Bring to the boil and pour half over the chicken. Bake uncovered, in a moderately hot oven for about 40 minutes basting occasionlly until tender; adjust seasonings. Meanwhile peel the pawpaw, remove the seeds and cut into slices. Poach gently in the remainder of the sauce together with the pepper for about 5 minutes. Arrange the chicken on a serving dish with the pawpaw and green pepper spooned around the edge.

Marinated Chicken with Mustard

Use a mild German mustard to flavour the sauce with the addition of soy sauce and pineapple.

Serves 4–5

12 chicken drumsticks or thighs 150 ml
(¼ pint) unsweetened pineapple juice
1–2 cloves garlic, crushed
3 tablespoons soy sauce

1 level tablespoon German mustard
salt and pepper
3 level tablespoons redcurrant jelly
fresh pineapple to garnish

Preparation time: 15 minutes, plus marinating time
Cooking time: 20 minutes

Lay the pieces of chicken in a shallow dish in a single layer. Combine the pineapple juice, garlic, soy sauce, mustard and seasonings and pour over the chicken. Cover and chill for 12–24 hours, turning once if possible. To serve: drain off the marinade into a saucepan, add the redcurrant jelly and heat until dissoved, then boil until reduced to a thin glaze. Cool a little. Arrange the chicken in a foil–lined grill pan and brush with the marinade glaze. Cook under a moderate heat 5–8 minutes, turn over and glaze again; continue to cook for 5–8 minutes until well browned and cooked through. Serve hot or cold with wedges of fresh pineapple to garnish.

Red Chicken Curry

A curry made from the various spices with a tomato flavouring.

Serves 4

1.75 kg (4 lb) oven ready chicken
425 g (15 oz) can tomatoes
40 g (1½ oz) butter or margarine
1 large onion, peeled and sliced
large pinch crushed dried chillies
1 level teaspoon grated raw root ginger
    or 1 level teaspoon ground ginger

¼ level teaspoon chilli seasoning or mild
    chilli powder
pinch of ground cloves
½ level teaspoon ground cinnamon
8 cardamom seeds, crushed
½ level teaspoon turmeric
4 tablespoons chicken stock or water
1 level teaspoon salt

Preparation time: 15 minutes
Cooking time: 1 hour
Heat the oven to 180°C/350°F/Gas Mark 4.

Cut the chicken into 8 pieces. Liquidize or purée the tomatoes. Heat the butter or margarine in a large frying pan and fry the chicken pieces until browned; remove from the pan. Fry the onion in the same fat until soft, then add the puréed tomatoes and all the spices, stock and salt. Bring to the boil and simmer gently for 10 minutes. Add the pieces of chicken, coat well in the sauce then cover and simmer very gently for 40–45 minutes or until tender. Alternatively cook in a moderate oven for 45–50 minutes until tender. Serve with boiled rice, poppadums, farmhouse yogurt, mango or peach chutney and chopped cucumber as accompaniments.

Freezing recommended: *for up to 1 month. Thaw completely before cooking.*

Chicken en Cocotte

A pot roasted chicken flavoured with salami, herbs and red peppers.

Serves 6

1.8–2.25 kg (4–5 lb) oven ready chicken
1 clove garlic, crushed
salt and pepper
2 tablespoons oil
1 onion, peeled and sliced
50 g (2 oz) salami, finely chopped
1 red pepper, deseeded and sliced

3–4 carrots, peeled and sliced
250 ml (8 fl oz) chicken stock
4 tablespoons dry white wine
1 level teaspoon mixed herbs or tarragon
parsley to garnish
2 level teaspoons cornflour (optional)

Preparation time: *15 minutes*
Cooking time: *1½ hours*
Heat the oven to 190°C/375°F/Gas Mark 5.

Rub the chicken all over with crushed garlic and put the remainder inside the cavity. Season the bird all over. Heat the oil in a large frying pan and fry the chicken carefully until golden brown. Transfer to a large casserole and arrange the onion, salami, red pepper around the bird. Combine the stock, wine, seasonings and herbs, bring to the boil and pour over the chicken. Cover the casserole with a lid or foil and cook in a moderately hot oven for about 1½ hours or until tender. Remove the lid for the last 15 minutes. Transfer the chicken to a serving dish and garnish with parsley. Put the juices from the casserole into a saucepan and skim off any fat. If liked, thicken with the cornflour blended in a little cold water, bring back to the boil and season to taste. Serve the chicken.

Freezing recommended: *for up 2 months. Thaw completely before re–cooking.*

Normandy Chicken

This recipe is based on a classic French dish where the chicken is cooked on a bed of apples flavoured with calvados and cream.

Serves 4–6

1.8 kg (4 lb) oven ready chicken (or guinea fowl)
1 lemon, quartered
salt and pepper

75 g (3 oz) butter or margarine
675 g (1½ lb) cooking apples
3–4 tablespoons calvados or brandy
6–8 tablespoons single cream

To garnish:
chopped fresh herbs
watercress

Preparation time: *20 minutes*
Cooking time: *1½ hours*
Heat the oven to 200°C/400°F/Gas Mark 6.

Prepare the bird and place the lemon in the cavity. If liked, season lightly all over and then rub the skin with a little of the softened butter. Peel, core and slice the apples and arrange about ⅔ of them in a lightly greased, fairly shallow ovenproof dish. Place the chicken on top and arrange the rest of the apples around the bird. Melt the remaining butter and brush over the apples. Cover with foil and cook in a fairly hot oven for an hour. Remove the foil, pour the calvados or brandy over the chicken and the cream over the apples. Return to the oven and cook, uncovered, for about 30 minutes more until well browned and cooked through. Carefully transfer the chicken to a serving dish and spoon the apples and juices around the bird. Sprinkle with chopped mixed herbs and garnish with plenty of watercress.

Turkey Boulangère

This recipe uses the thigh meat of the turkey which is now readily available both fresh and frozen; and is layered with a tangy pâté stuffing before braising.

Serves 6

3–4 turkey thigh joints, boneless or
boned, aprox 900 g (2 lb)
salt and pepper
175 g (6 oz) coarse liver pâté
3 level tablespoons cranberry and
orange sauce
25 g (1 oz) fresh breadcrumbs

25 g (1 oz) butter or margarine
900 g (2 lb) potatoes, peeled thinly
sliced
2 onions, peeled and thinly sliced
150 ml (¼ pint) white wine or stock
6 tomatoes
chopped parsley to garnish

Preparation time: *25 minutes*
Cooking time: *2 hours*
Heat the oven to 180°C/350°F/Gas Mark 4.

Remove the skin from all but one of the pieces of turkey. Lay the thighs out and season well. Combine the pâté, cranberry sauce, breadcrumbs and seasonings and spread over two or three pieces of the turkey. Layer up to look like one joint, keeping the piece with the skin on top; secure with string. Brown the joint all over and then remove from the pan. Arrange the sliced potatoes and onions in a greased roasting tin or large casserole, seasoning with salt and pepper as you go. Place the joint in the centre of the potatoes and pour the wine or stock over it. Cover with foil or a lid and cook in a moderate oven for 1½ hours.

Remove the foil, cut a cross in each tomato and arrange around the turkey on top of the potatoes. Increase the temperature to fairly hot (200°C/400°F/Gas Mark 6) and return to the oven for about 30 minutes or until the turkey is cooked through. Remove the string and serve sprinkled with chopped parsley, sliced so each portion recieves potatoes, a tomato and juices from the dish.

Freezing recommended; *for up to 2 months. Thaw completely before re–cooking.*

Turkey Escalopes Stilton

Turkey is so versatile and here it blends well with the tangy flavour of Stilton.

Serves 4

4 fillets escalopes or fillets
50 g (2 oz) Stilton cheese
approx 2 level tablespoons seasoned
*   flour*
50 g (2 oz) butter or margarine
2 tablespoons oil
1 small onion, peeled and very finely
*   chopped*
300 ml (½ pint) chicken stock

3–4 tablespoons medium sherry
1 tablespoon lemon juice
1 level teaspoon finely chopped gherkins
salt and pepper

To garnish:
watercress
gherkin fans

Preparation time: *15 minutes*
Cooking time: *20 minutes*

If using frozen turkey make sure it is completely thawed. Using a sharp knife, make a pocket in each fillet. Divide the crumbled Stilton cheese between the fillets, securing each with a wooden cocktail stick. Dip the escalopes in seasoned flour to coat thoroughly. Fry in a mixture of the melted fat and oil for about 5 minutes on each side or until golden brown or cooked through. Drain on absorbent paper and keep warm. Pour off all but one tablespoon fat from the pan and fry the onion until soft. Stir in the remaining seasoned flour, cook for 1 minute then gradually add the stock and sherry and bring to the boil for 2 minutes. Sharpen with lemon juice, stir in the chopped gherkins and season to taste; replace the turkey and simmer for 2–3 minutes. Arrange the turkey on a serving dish, spoon the sauce over and garnish with watercress and gherkin fans.

Turkey Carbonnade

Sometimes you can buy turkey casserole meat, if not available use thigh meat and cut into cubes yourself.

Serves 4–5

675 g (1½ lb) turkey casserole meat or
boneless thigh meat
2 tablespoons oil or dripping
1 large onion, peeled and sliced
1 clove garlic, crushed
100 g (4 oz) carrots, peeled and sliced
25 g (1 oz) flour
300 ml (½ pint) brown ale

150 ml (¼ pint) chicken stock
2 teaspoons vinegar
1 level teaspoon brown sugar
1½ level teaspoons tomato purée
good dash of Worcestershire sauce
1 bay leaf
100 g (4 oz) button mushrooms, halved

Preparation time: *20 minutes*
Cooking time: *1 hour*
Heat the oven to 160°C/325°F/Gas Mark 3.

Trim the turkey and if using thigh meat cut into 2.5 cm (1 inch) cubes. Heat the oil in a pan and fry the turkey until lightly browned all over. Transfer to a casserole. Fry the onion and garlic in the remaining fat in the pan until soft. Add the carrots and continue for about 2 minutes. Stir in the flour, cook for a minute or so then gradually add the ale and stock and bring to the boil, stirring continuously. Add the vinegar, sugar, tomato purée, Worcestershire sauce and bay leaf; season well and pour over the turkey. Cover and cook in a moderate oven for about 45 minutes. Adjust seasonings, add the mushrooms and return to the oven for 15–20 minutes or until tender. Discard the bay leaf and serve with buttered noodles, rice or jacket potatoes.

Freezing recommended: *for up to 2 months. Thaw completely before re–cooking.*

Oxtail Casserole

A good economical dish full of vegetables and flavour.

Serves 4–5

1 oxtail, cut up
2 tablespoons oil
25 g (1 oz) flour 150 ml (¼ pint) red or
white wine or cider
450 ml (¾ pint) stock or water
2 large onions, peeled and chopped
4 carrots, peeled and sliced
3–4 sticks celery, sliced

salt and pepper
1 level teaspoon each paprika, curry
powder and Worcestershire sauce
2 bay leaves
16 black olives
freshly chopped mixed herbs or parsley
to garnish

Preparation time: *25 minutes*
Cooking time: *4 hours*
Heat the oven to 160°C/325°F/Gas mark 3.

Trim any excess fat from the pieces of oxtail then brown each piece throughly in the heated oil. Remove from the pan, pour off all but 1½ table-spoons fat from the pan, stir in the flour and cook for a minute or so. Gradually add the wine (or cider) and stock and bring to the boil. Add the onions, carrots and celery, plenty of seasonings, paprika, curry powder and Worcestershire sauce. Replace the oxtail, add the bay leaves and the olives and cover tightly. Either simmer very gently for about 3 hours; or transfer to an ovenproof casserole and cook in a very moderate oven for 3½–4 hours or until very tender. It may be necessary to add a little extra boiling stock or water to the casserole.

If possible cool the casserole, chill over night, then lift off the layer of fat on the surface. Discard the bay leaves. Reheat thoroughly either by bringing to the boil and simmering for 20 minutes or by cooking in a moderate oven for an hour. Serve sprinkled with herbs or parsley.

Freezing recommended: *for up to 2 months, thaw completely before re–cooking.*

Roast Duck with Spiced Pears

Use either a whole duck or portions for this recipe.

Serves 4

1 onion, peeled and finely chopped
2 cloves garlic, crushed
2.5 cm (1 inch) piece fresh root ginger,
*   peeled and chopped*
150 ml (¼ pint) red wine
1 level tablespoon caster sugar
¾ level teaspoon five–spice powder
or ½ level teaspoon ground allspice
2 bay leaves, preferably fresh

salt and pepper
4 ripe pears
1.8 kg (4 lb) duckling or 4 breast por-
*   tions of duck*
1 level teaspoon cornflour

To garnish:
fresh bay leaves
parsley

Preparation time: *30 minutes*
Cooking time: *45 minutes – 1¼ hours*
Heat the oven to 220°C/425°F/Gas Mark 7.

Put the onion, garlic, ginger, wine, sugar, spice powder or allspice, bay leaves, salt and pepper into a bowl. Peel, core and quarter the pears or if large cut into eighths. Add to the marinade, mix well and leave for about an hour. Transfer to a saucepan, cover and simmer very gently for about 20 minutes,turning several times, until the pears turn translucent. Meanwhile, if cooking a whole duck, prick the skin all over and stand on a rack in a roasting tin. If using breasts just prick the skin – it is not necessary to stand them on a rack. Season lightly, if liked. Cook in a hot oven allowing about 1¼ hours for a whole bird or about 40–45 minutes for the portions. If liked, baste just once during cooking. Drain off all the fat and arrange the duck portions on a serving dish.

Reheat the pears and arrange around the bird. Strain the marinade into a clean pan and, if necessary, add a little stock. Thicken with cornflour blended with a little cold water, bring back to the boil and adjust the seasonings. Serve the duck, garnished with fresh bay leaves and parsley.

Pheasant with Walnuts and Cranberries

A good recipe to use equally well with young or mature birds.

Serves 4

1 tablespoon oil 25 g (1 oz) butter or margarine
1–2 mature pheasants, oven ready
salt and pepper
1 large onion, peeled and sliced
4–5 sticks of celery, sliced

1½ level tablespoons flour
approx. 300 ml (½ pint) stock
150 ml (¼ pint) dry white wine
75 g (3 oz) whole cranberries, fresh or frozen
50 g (2 oz) walnut halves

Preparation time: 20 minutes
Cooking time: 1¼ hours
Heat the oven to 180°C/350°F/Gas Mark 4.

Melt the oil and butter in a pan. Cut the pheasant into quarters and season well. Fry quickly in the fat until browned all over, then place in a casserole. Fry the onion and celery gently in the same fat until soft, but not coloured. Stir in the flour and cook for a minute or so. Gradually add the stock and wine and bring to the boil. Season well and pour over the pheasant. Cover the casserole and cook in a moderate oven for 45 minutes. Adjust the seasonings, stir in the cranberries, walnuts and a little more boiling stock if necessary, then replace the lid and return to the oven for 20–30 minutes, or until very tender.

Freezing recommended: for up to 2 months. Thaw completely before re–cooking.

Game Pie

No collection of recipes which includes game would be complete without a game pie.

Serves 8–10

225 g (8 oz) raw pie veal or lean bone-
    less pork
225 g (8 oz) cooked ham
1 small onion, peeled
salt and pepper

Hot Water Crust Pastry:
450 g (1 lb) plain flour
1 level teaspoon salt
100 g (4 oz) lard
200 ml (7 fl oz) water; or milk and
    water mixed

good pinch of ground mace or nutmeg
approx 350 g (12 oz) cooked game (e.g.
    pheasant, grouse, hare, venison, wild
    duck etc.; or a mixture)

beaten egg to glaze
2 level teaspoons powdered gelatine
300 ml (½ pint) game stock (made from
    the carcass)
salads to garnish

Preparation time: 1 hour
Cooking time: 1½ hours
Heat the oven to 200°C/400°F/Gas Mark 6.

Mince the veal, ham and onion and mix in plenty of seasonings and the mace. *For the pastry:* sift the flour and salt into a bowl. Melt the lard in the water and bring to the boil. Pour in the boiling liquid onto the flour and quickly mix to form a smooth dough, kneading as necessary. Roll out about ¾ of the pastry into a circle large enough to line a lightly greased game pie mould or 18–20 cm (7–8 inch) round cake tin, preferably with a loose base, or a 900 g (2 lb) loaf tin. Meanwhile, cover the rest of the pastry in the bowl. Position the pastry carefully in the tin, making sure it fits into the corners.

Lay half the minced meats in the tin, cover with chopped game and then with the rest of the meats. Roll out the reserved pastry to make a lid, dampen the edges and position. Press the edges well together, trim and crimp. Use the trimmings to make leaves to decorate the top of the pie. Make a hole in the centre and glaze the pastry. Cook in a fairly hot oven for 30 minutes, then glaze again. Cook for a further hour covering with grease proof paper when sufficiently brown. Dissolve the gelatine in the stock, season and as the pie cools, pour the liquid into it through the central hole using a small funnel. Leave for about 10 minutes for the stock to sink down, then add some more. Cool completely, then chill, at least overnight. Turn out, garnish with salads and serve into slices.

Venison Casserole

Now that venison is so much more widely available, take advantage of the fact and try it. As it has virtually no fat, it is excellent for those who are calorie counting. This recipe can also be used for a pie, by topping it with either puff or shortcrust pastry.

Serves 4

675 g (1–1½ lb) casserole or stewing
   venison, boned
450 ml (¾ pint) red wine
2 cloves garlic, crushed
2 bay leaves, preferably fresh
2 strips orange rind
2 strips lemon rind
2 tablespoons lemon juice
8 whole cloves
2–3 tablespoons oil

100 g (4 oz) piece streaky bacon,
   derinded and diced
12 button onions, peeled or 2 onions,
   peeled and sliced
1 level tablespoon flour
salt and pepper
little stock
100 g (4 oz) cranberries, fresh or frozen
3 level tablespoons redcurrant or rowan
   jelly

Preparation time: *25 minutes*
Cooking time: *1¾ –2hrs*

Cut the venison into 2.5 cm (1 inch) cubes and place in a bowl. Combine the wine, garlic, bay leaves, fruit rinds, lemon juice, cloves and 1–2 tablespoons oil, pour over the venison, cover and leave in a cool place to marinate for 12–24 hours, giving an occasional stir.

Strain the marinade and reserve with the bay leaves. Heat the remaining oil in a pan and fry the bacon and onions until lightly browned. Transfer to a casserole. Add the venison to a pan and fry until well sealed. Transfer it to the casserole. Sprinkle the flour over the contents of the pan, cook for a minute or so then gradually add the reserved marinade. Bring to boil and season well. Pour over the venison, adding the bay leaves from the marinade, then cover and cook in a very moderate oven for an hour. Remove the lid, add extra boiling stock if necessary and stir in the cranberries; stir in the jelly until dissolved. Replace the lid and return to the oven for a further ¾–1 hour until really tender. Discard bay leaves and adjust the seasonings. Serve with jacket or scallopped potatoes and braised celery or fennel.

Freezing recommended: *for up to 2 months. Thaw completely before re–cooking.*

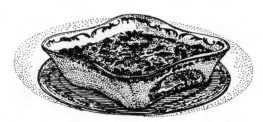

Rabbit Casserole

You can buy ready diced boneless rabbit, if this isn't available, use rabbit portions and bone and dice them before use.

Serves 4

*100 g (4 oz) streaky bacon, derinded
    and chopped
1 tablespoon oil
12 button onions, peeled or 1 onion,
    peeled and sliced
1 clove garlic, crushed
675 g (1½ lb) boneless, diced rabbit
150 ml (¼ pint) cider
450 ml (¾ pint) stock*

*salt and pepper
grated rind of 1 orange
8–12 no–need–to–soak prunes
1 bay leaf
good pinch ground nutmeg
2–3 level teaspoons cornflour
3 tablespoons single cream (optional)
1 level tablespoon toasted sesame seeds*

Preparation time: *20 minutes*
Cooking time: *45 minutes*
Heat the oven to 180°C/350°F/Gas Mark 4.

Heat the bacon in a saucepan until the fat runs, then add the oil, onions and garlic and continue cooking until they begin to colour a little. Add the rabbit and mix well, then cook until lightly sealed, stirring frequently. Add the cider and stock and bring to the boil. Season, then stir in the orange rind, prunes, bay leaf and nutmeg. Cover and simmer for about 40 minutes, alternatively transfer to a casserole and cook in a moderate oven for about the same time. Discard the bay leaf and thicken with the cornflour blended with the cream or a little cold water. Bring back to the boil until thickened, adjust the seasonings and serve sprinkled with toasted sesame seeds. Braised red cabbage and cream potatoes make good accompaniments.

Freezing recommended: *for up to 2 months. Thaw completely before re–cooking.*

PUDDINGS AND DESSERTS

INTRODUCTION

After the main course comes a craving for a pudding of some type. Hot puddings for the winter, cold desserts for the summer, dinner parties, buffet tables and more elegant eating. There is nothing better to come home to on a cold winter's day than a piping hot pudding. Some hot puddings such as Crêpes Suzette are the ultimate in elegance whilst something such as Orange and Lemon Pudding or Treacle Tart will tempt most palates; and a steamed pudding with layers of fruit is hard to beat.

Cold desserts tend to be good to serve when time is short or the rest of the meal requires a lot of attention, for many can be prepared in advance, often up to 24 hours or more – and the scope is enormous. Ice creams, sorbets, trifles, soufflés, fruit salads, syllabubs just to name a few, and all comparatively easy to prepare.

Puddings and desserts always conjure up the thought of an abundance of calories and indeed this is the case with some of the pastry or sponge–based recipes and those full of cream such as syllabubs, soufflés and trifles. However there are also many dishes suitable for those trying to keep their calorie and cholesterol levels low – particularly recipes based on yogurt instead of cream or those which use fruit.

Cream is a major ingredient in many recipes and it is important to buy the right type. When using cream for whipping it should be double or whipping cream only; single, half and half and other thinner creams do not contain enough fat for it to whip satisfactorily, so they should be used only for pouring. Double cream can be 'watered down' or extended with milk or wine (as in syllabubs) and will still whip satisfactorily by adding 2 tablespoons to each 150 ml (¼ pint) cream. Take care not to over whip cream or it will curdle and then separate out and although it will still taste all right the texture will be ruined, making it impossible to use. Whilst whipping, stop from time to time to check and use at the 'floppy' or soft peak stage for spreading and adding to soufflés, ice cream etc., when it will fold into the mixture much more easily. When piping, complete the last stage very carefully and remember that the cream thickens a little more as it is squeezed from the piping bag.

Apple and Pear Pudding

A lovely warming steamed pudding, mingling the flavours of apples and pears.

Serves 4–5

225 g (8 oz) pears
350 g (12 oz) cooking apples
2–3 tablespoons sugar
100 g (4 oz) soft margarine
100 g (4 oz) caster or light soft brown
    sugar
2 eggs (size 2 or 3)
grated rind of ½ lemon
few drops almond essence (optional)
100 g (4 oz) self–raising flour

½ level teaspoon baking powder

Almond Sauce:
2 eggs
300 ml (½ pint) milk
1 level teaspoon cornflour
½ teaspoon almond essence
approx. 25 g (1 oz) sugar
25 g (1 oz) flaked almonds, toasted and
    chopped

Preparation time: *20 minutes*
Cooking time: *2 hours*

Peel the pears and apples, remove cores and slice thinly. Put into a basin and mix with the sugar. *For the sponge:* place margarine, sugar, eggs, lemon rind and essence in a bowl. Sift in the flour and baking powder and beat together thoroughly for 2 minutes. Grease a 1.2–1.5 litre (2–2½ pint) pudding basin and spread a layer of sponge mixture in the base. Cover with a layer of fruit and then spread with a second layer of sponge. Add the rest of the fruit and cover with the remaining sponge mixture. Level the top, cover with a piece of greased greaseproof paper with a pleat across the centre and then with a similar cover of foil; secure tightly around the edge with string. Place in a saucepan with boiling water coming half-way up the side of the basin and simmer gently for 2 hours, adding more boiling water to the pan as necessary.

For the sauce: put the beaten eggs, milk and cornflour in the top of a double saucepan or basin over a pan of gently simmering water until thickened, stirring frequently. Add essence, sugar to taste and just before serving stir in the chopped nuts. Turn the pudding out carefully and serve with the warm sauce.

Hot Fruit Soufflé

To serve as one large soufflé or individual ones, the base of fruit gives added interest to a liqueur flavoured soufflé mixture.

Serves 6

425 g (15 oz) can raspberries, apricots,
    peaches, pears etc; or a mixture of
    fresh fruit, sliced

40 g (1½ oz) butter
4 level tablespoons flour
300 ml (½ pint) milk

50 g (2 oz) caster sugar

4 eggs, separated

1 tablespoon brandy or liqueur

icing sugar for dredging

Preparation time: 20 minutes

Cooking time: 25–45 minutes

Heat the oven to 180°C/350°F/Gas Mark 4.

Grease a soufflé dish of 18 cm (7 inch) approx 1.7 litres (3 pints) or six fairly large individual soufflé dishes. Lay the drained and sliced fruit in the base of the dish or dishes. Melt the butter in a saucepan, stir in the flour and cook for a minute or so until bubbling. Gradually add the milk and stir until smooth, then allow to come to the boil, stirring frequently, and simmer for 1–2 minutes. Remove from the heat and beat in the sugar, until dissolved, followed by the egg yolks and liqueur. Whisk the egg whites until very stiff and standing in peaks. Beat 2 tablespoons into the sauce and then fold in the remainder evenly. Pour into the prepared dish and bake in a fairly hot oven for about 40–45 minutes for the large soufflé; or 20–30 minutes for the small ones, until well risen and golden brown. Serve immediately, lightly sprinkled with sifted icing sugar.

Christmas Pudding

This recipe has been in my family for as long as we can remember, and it is extra moist because it uses only breadcrumbs, no flour.

Makes 2 approx. 900 g (2 lb) puddings

225 g (8 oz) sultanas

225 g (8 oz) currants

225 g (8 oz) seedless raisins

225 g (8 oz) stoned raisins, chopped

100 g (4 oz) cut mixed peel

200 g (4 oz) glacé cherries, chopped

100 g (4 oz) blanched almonds, chopped

100 g (4 oz) ground almonds

225 g (8 oz) fresh breadcrumbs, brown
  or white

1 large carrot, peeled and finely grated

225 g (8 oz) shredded suet

1 large apple, peeled, cored and grated

½ level teaspoon ground cinnamon

1 level teaspoon mixed spice

¼ level teaspoon ground allspice

225 g (8 oz) demerara or soft brown
  sugar

grated rind and juice of 1 lemon

grated rind and juice of 1 orange

4 eggs (size 2 or 3), beaten

6 tablespoons brandy

approx 150 ml (¼ pint) brown ale or
  sherry

lard or white fat for greasing the basins

Preparation time: 45 minutes

Cooking time: 8 hours plus 4 hours

Put all the ingredients into a large mixing bowl in the order in which they are listed and mix very well together. Grease two 1.2 litre (2 pint) basins liberally with lard and spoon in the mixture. Cover the basins first with a double layer of well greased greaseproof paper and then with a pudding cloth or foil. Tie securely in place. Place each pudding in a saucepan with boiling water coming half-way up the sides of the basins. Cover and simmer gently for 7–8 hours, adding extra boiling water as necessary. Remove puddings and leave until completely cold. Remove the covers from the puddings and, if liked, pierce all over and add 2 tablespoons brandy to each one. Cover with fresh greased greaseproof and a cloth or foil and store in a cool dry place until required. Boil as above for 3–4 hours before serving with brandy or rum butter, or cream.

For pressure cooking: follow the instructions given by the manufacturers.

For oven cooking: stand the basins in a roasting tin and pour boiling water around them so there is at least 4 cm (1½ inches) water in the tin. Cover the whole tin with foil, carefully sealing it under the edges. Cook in a cool oven (150°C/300°F/Gas Mark 2) for 8 hours. Check after 5–6 hours to see if any more boiling water should be added to the tin.

Brandy Butter – This can be made up to a month in advance and kept in the freezer; or kept in the refrigerator for 7–10 days if kept in a covered container.

175 g (6 oz) unsalted butter	*finely grated rind of ½ orange (optional)*
approx. 225 g (8 oz) icing sugar, sifted	*2 tablespoons brandy or rum*

Cream the butter until light and fluffy and gradually add the icing sugar, beating it in smoothly and adding orange rind (if used) and brandy as you go. Adjust the icing sugar content to obtain the desired consistency.

Coffee Walnut Crêpes

Quick and easy to prepare if you make the pancakes in advance; they can be stored in the refrigerator for 2–3 days before use.

Serves 4

Batter:
100 g (4 oz) plain flour
pinch salt
2 eggs (size 2 or 3)
275 ml (scant ½ pint) milk
40 g (1½ oz) walnut halves, finely
  chopped
oil or lard for frying

Sauce:
40 g (1½ oz) butter

Preparation time: *25 minutes*
Cooking time: *20 minutes*

3 level tablespoons caster sugar
250 ml (8 fl oz) strong black coffee
juice of 1 orange
2 tablespoons brandy, Tia Maria or
  orange liqueur

To decorate:
whipped cream
julienne strips of orange rind
walnut halves

For the pancakes: sift the flour and salt into a bowl and make a well in the centre. Add the eggs and a little milk and graually work in the flour, adding more milk as necessary. Add the remaining milk and beat until smooth; then beat in the walnuts. Heat a little oil or lard in a small frying pan (approx. 20 cm/ 8 inch) and pour in sufficient batter to cover the base. Cook for a minute or so until lightly browned; turn over and cook the second side. Remove from the pan and make seven more in the same way. Store if necessary with strips of paper between each and wrapped in foil in the refrigerator.

For the sauce: melt the butter in a large frying pan then add the sugar, mix in and cook until caramelized. Add the black coffee and cook until the caramel has melted, then add the orange juice. Add one pancake to the pan and fold it into four so the sauce coats it completely; remove to a plate and repeat with the other 7. Return all the pancakes to the pan then add the brandy or liqueur. If using brandy, ignite it. Serve 2 pancakes per serving with sauce spooned over and topped with a spoonful of cream, strips of orange rind and walnuts.

Bread, Butter and Apple Pudding

A variation of the old favourite with apples and fruit rinds added for extra succulence. The bread may also be spread with chunky marmalade if liked.

Serves 4–5

4–5 slices bread (brown or white)
50 g (2 oz) butter
100 g (4 oz) mixed dried fruit
25 g (1 oz) mixed peel
grated rind of 1 orange or lemon

2 cooking apples, peeled, cored and sliced
75 g (3 oz) demerara sugar
3 eggs (size 2 or 3)
450–568 ml (¾–1 pint) milk
little mixed spice or ground cinnamon

Preparation time: *15 minutes*
Cooking time: *1 hour*
Heat the oven to 190°C/375°F/Gas Mark 5.

Spread the bread with most of the butter; use the remainder to grease a 1 litre (2 pint) ovenproof dish. Cut the bread into strips and arrange in layers alternating with dried fruit, peel, fruit rind, apples and most of the sugar. Beat the eggs and milk together and strain into the dish. Leave to stand for at least 15 minutes and up to 1 hour, then sprinkle with spice and the remaining sugar. Cook in a moderately hot oven for about an hour or until well risen, set and golden brown. Serve hot either as it is or with cream.

Crêpes Suzette

A really delicious dessert for a really special occasion; much easier to make than many may think.

Serves 4

100 g (4 oz) plain flour
pinch of salt
2 eggs (size 2 or 3)
275 ml (scant ½ pint) milk
lard, butter or oil for frying

Sauce:
3 large oranges

1 lemon
100 g (4 oz) caster sugar
100 g (4 oz) butter
2 tablespoons Curaçao or other orange
  liqueur
3–4 tablespoons brandy

Preparation time: *20 minutes*
Cooking time: *20 minutes*

For the batter: sift the flour and salt into a bowl, make a well in the centre and add the eggs. Add a little of the milk and gradually work the flour into the liquid using a wooden spoon, spatula or flat hand whisk. Beat until smooth then gradually add the rest of the milk. Heat a knob of fat or a little oil in a small frying pan until really hot, swirling it around the pan. Pour in about 2 tablespoons batter and twist the pan around until the batter forms a thin skin all over the base of the pan. Cook for 1–2 minutes, over a moderate heat until the underside is lightly browned. Turn over and cook the second side lightly. Turn on to a plate. Make 7 more pancakes in the same way, layering them up with a disc of greaseproof paper between each one.

For the sauce: using a potato peeler, thinly pare the rind from one orange, cut into julienne strips and cook in boiling water for 5 minutes. Drain. Grate the rind from the second orange and the lemon. Squeeze the juice from the oranges and mix with 1 tablespoon juice from the lemon. Put the sugar into a large heavy–based frying pan and heat gently until it melts and begins to turn a light brown. Add the butter quickly and allow to melt, off the heat. Add the grated fruit rinds and juices and heat gently to allow the caramel to dissolve, then add the Curaçao or orange liqueur. Add the crepes, one at a time, dipping one side into the sauce then folding into quarters. Arrange the folded pancakes evenly in the sauce in the pan and sprinkle with strips of orange rind. Simmer for a couple of minutes spooning the juices over the pancakes. Pour over the warmed brandy and ignite. Serve as soon as the flames begin to subside.

Orange and Lemon Pudding

A surprising pudding which separates out during cooking to a featherlight sponge on top and a tangy fruit sauce underneath.

Serves 5–6

100 g (4 oz) soft margarine
225 g (8 oz) caster sugar
4 eggs, separated
grated rind of 1 large lemon

grated rind of 1 large orange
6 tablespoons lemon juice
100 g (4 oz) self-raising flour
568ml (1 pint) milk

Preparation time: 15 minutes
Cooking time: 1 hour
Heat the oven to 190°C/375°F/Gas Mark 5.

Beat the margarine and sugar until smooth. Beat in the egg yolks followed by the fruit rinds and lemon juice, and then beat in the flour. Mix in the milk until smooth and finally fold in the stiffly beaten egg whites. Quickly pour into a greased ovenproofed dish (approx 1.5 litres/3 pints) and stand in a roasting tin containing about 2.5 cm (1 inch) hot water. Cook in a moderately hot oven for 50–60 minutes or until firm to the touch with a light golden brown crust. Serve at once.

Note: do not worry if the mixture looks curdled this is normal.

Apple Strudel

A firm favourite with everyone, especially when it is made properly.

Serves 10–12

Strudel Pastry:
225 g (8 oz) plain flour
good pinch of salt

1 egg (size 2 or 3), beaten
2 tablespoons oil
4 tablespoons warm water

Filling:
900 g (2 lb) cooking apples
50 g (2 oz) currants
50 g (2 oz) raisins
grated rind of 1 lemon
100 g (4 oz) caster sugar

½ level teaspoon ground cinnamon or
mixed spice
75 g (3 oz) butter
100 g (4 oz) ground almonds
icing sugar for dredging

Preparation time: 1 hour, plus resting time
Cooking time: 40 minutes
Heat the oven to 190°C/37° F/Gas Mark 5.

Sift the flour and salt into a bowl and make a well in the centre. Add the beaten egg, oil and water and mix thoroughly to make a soft, sticky but pliable dough. Turn out and knead by hand for 12–15 minutes or in a large electric mixer fitted with a dough hook for about 5 minutes, until smooth, silky and even. Shape into a ball and place into a lightly oiled polythene bag. Leave to rest in a warm place for about an hour.

Spread out two clean tea towels side by side on a table with the long edges together, and slightly sprinkle with sifted flour. Place the dough in the centre and, using a warmed rolling pin, carefully roll it out to a rectangle about 45 x 30 cm (18 x 12 inches) and about 3 mm (⅛ inch) thick, lifting it occasionally to prevent sticking. Gently put your hands under the dough and working from centre outwards, use the backs of your hands to stretch the dough very carefully until it is thin enough to read a newspaper through. Take care not to tear it. The pastry should reach approx 90 x 70 cm (36 x 28 inches) and it must cover the cloths completely. Leave it to rest for 15 minutes.

For the filling: core and slice the apples very thinly into a bowl. Add the currants, raisins and lemon rind then mix in the sugar and spice. Trim off the thick edges of the pastry then cut the piece in half between the cloths. Melt the butter and brush it all over the surface of the pastry then sprinkle evenly with the ground almonds. Spoon the filling in a 10 cm (5 inch) wide strip along the edge of both pieces of pastry nearest to you, leaving a margin of about 5 cm (2 inches) at each side. Turn the side edges over the filling to keep it in place. Then, using both hands, lift the cloth, flip the end of the pastry over the filling and begin to roll it up. Pull the cloth and the dough towards you and gently lift the cloth a little at a time to help the dough roll over. Continue until it is completely rolled up. Roll the second strudel in the same way. Carefully turn the strudels onto greased baking sheets with the seam underneath and brush the tops with more melted butter. Cook just above the centre of a moderately hot oven for 35–40 minutes until golden brown. Remove very carefully from the baking sheet to a serving dish and serve dusted with icing sugar and cut into slices as required. Serve hot or cold.

Old Fashioned Treacle Tart

Originally treacle and syrup tart was made using brown treacle, dried fruits, peeled and fruit slices; and this is a variation on that theme.

Serves 6

100 g (4 oz) plain flour
pinch of salt
25 g (1 oz) butter or block margarine
25 g (1 oz) lard or white fat
water to mix

Filling:
6 tablespoons golden syrup
2 tablespoons black treacle

50 g (2 oz) raisins
25 g (1 oz) cut mixed peel
25 g (1 oz) shelled walnuts, roughly
chopped
finely grated rind of ½ lemon
finely grated rind of ½ orange
good pinch of ground allspice
50 g (2 oz) fresh breadcrumbs

Preparation time: *20 minutes*
Cooking time: *25–30 minutes*
Heat the oven to 200°C/400°F/Gas Mark 6.

Make up the pastry as for shortcrust pastry (see page 26). Roll out and use to line a 20 cm (8 inch) deep pie plate or flan dish. Gently warm the syrup and treacle together. Sprinkle the raisins, peel and walnuts into the pastry case and sprinkle with the fruit rinds and allspice. Pour over the warmed syrup and treacle, then sprinkle with the breadcrumbs, leaving for a few minutes to settle and soak in. Cook in a fairly hot oven for about 25 minutes or until the filling is firm and the pastry lightly browned.

Coffee Syllabubs

An unexpected crunchy base and kiwi fruit add interest to this delicious syllabub.

Serves 4

16 ratafia biscuits
2 kiwi fruits
5 tablespoons very strong black coffee,
  warmed
5 level teaspoons caster sugar

¼ level teaspoon ground cinnamon
2 tablespoons brandy or Tia Maria
450 ml (¾ pint) double cream
coffee–flavoured chocolate matchsticks
  to decorate

Preparation time: 20 minutes

Roughly break up the ratafias and divide between 4 glasses. Peel and slice the kiwi fruit and reserve the eight best slices for decoration. Cut the remainder in half and mix with the ratafias. Put the coffee into a large bowl and stir in the sugar until dissolved, then add the cinnamon and brandy or liqueur and leave until cold. Add the cream and whisk slowly until it thickens sufficiently to stand in soft peaks. Spoon or pipe over the biscuit base and chill until required. Decorate each portion with two slices of kiwi fruit and chocolate matchsticks.

Coffee Walnut Meringues

These meringues are light brown in colour with a gooey coffee and nut centre.

Makes 8–10

2 egg whites
150 g (5 oz) icing sugar, sifted
2 level teaspoons instant coffee powder
50 g (2 oz) walnut pieces, finely
  chopped

Topping:
150 ml (¼ pint) double cream
1 tablespoon milk or Tia Maria
8–10 strawberries

Preparation time: 20 minutes
Cooking time: 30–40 minutes
Heat the oven to 150°C/300°F/Gas Mark 2.

Cover two baking sheets with non–stick baking paper. Put the egg whites into a heatproof bowl with the icing sugar and stand it over a saucepan of gently simmering water. Whisk the mixture continuously until it thickens and stands in soft peaks, add the coffee and continue whisking until it stands in stiff peaks. Remove from the heat and beat in the nuts evenly. Spoon or pipe the mixture onto the baking sheet forming approx 6 cm (2½ inch) rounds. Cook in a cool oven for about 30 minutes or until crisp and easily moved from the paper. Leave to cool on the paper, then peel off and store in an airtight container. *To serve:* whip the cream with the milk or Tia Maria until stiff and either spread or pipe a whirl on top of each meringue. Top this with a whole or quartered strawberry.

Coffee Malakoff Cake

Ideal for a dinner party or luncheon as it is best made 24–48 hours in advance, leaving just the decoration to be completed on the day.

Serves 8–10

2 packets sponge finger biscuits
150 g (5 oz) blanched almonds, roughly
  chopped
100 g (4 oz) caster sugar
175 g (6 oz) butter
4 tablespoons milk
4 tablespoons Tia Maria or dark rum

4 tablespoons strong black coffee
300 ml (½ pint) whipping cream

To decorate:
Coffee–flavoured chocolate matchsticks
slivers of blanched almonds, toasted
glacé cherries

Preparation time: *45 minutes, plus chilling time*

Grease and line a 23 x 12.5 cm (9 x 5 inch) loaf tin, preferably using non–stick baking paper. Cover the base with sponge finger biscuits. Put the almonds and 50 g (2 oz) of the sugar in a small pan and heat gently until the sugar turns a light caramel colour. Turn on to an oiled baking sheet, leave until cold and then crush with a rolling pin or in the food processor. Cream the butter until soft then add the remaining sugar and beat in, followed by 1 tablespoon milk and 1½ tablespoons each of Tia Maria and black coffee; finally stir in the crushed nuts. Mix together the remaining milk, liqueur and coffee and sprinkle two tablespoons over the biscuits in the tin; then spread with half the nut mixture. Add a second layer of sponge fingers, sprinkle with half the remaining milk mixture and cover with the remaining nut butter. Lay a final layer of sponge fingers evenly on top and sprinkle with the rest of the milk mixture. Press down evenly and cover with non–stick baking paper and foil. If possible, place a light weight evenly over the gâteau, then chill for at least 12 hours and preferably for 24–48 hours.

To serve: gently turn out the gâteau onto a serving dish and peel off the paper. Whip the cream until stiff and use some of it to mask the whole gâteau, marking the sides attractively with a small palette knife or fork. Put the remainder into a piping bag fitted with a star nozzle and use to decorate the top and base of the gâteau, together with coffee matchsticks and halved glacé cherries. Sprinkle the toasted nuts in between the lines of cream. Serve in slices.

Strawberry and Orange Boodle

An old favourite which used to be served at the London club Boodles.

Serves 4

12 Boudoir biscuits or sponge fingers
300 ml (½ pint) soured cream
grated rind and juice of 2 oranges
2 teaspoons lemon juice
40 g (1½ oz) caster sugar

225 g (8 oz) strawberries, halved or
  quartered

To decorate:
orange slices
mint sprigs or lemon geranium leaves

Preparation time: 20 minutes, plus chilling time

Crumble one boudoir biscuit into the base of each of four fairly large glasses. Halve the remainder and put four halves down the sides of each glass. Turn the cream into a bowl and gradually mix in the grated orange rind and juice and the lemon juice, followed by the sugar. Mix in the strawberries and then divide the mixture between the glasses. Chill thoroughly for about 2 hours before serving, decorated with orange slices and a sprig of mint or lemon geranium leaves.

Note: you can substitute other fruit such as raspberries (and other berries) peaches, or apricots for the strawberries according to what is available. If preferred a mixture of half whipped double cream and half soured cream or yogurt may be used in place of the soured cream.

Yogurt Mousse with Stawberries and Redcurrant Sauce

A delicious Greek yogurt mousse set in glasses alternating with strawberries.

Serves 4–6

2 eggs
50 g (2 oz) caster sugar
200 ml (½ pint) milk
2 tablespoons white rum
1 tablespoon water
1 level tablespoon powdered gelatine
150 ml (¼ pint) Greek yogurt

75 g (6 oz) fresh strawberries

Redcurrant Sauce:
175 g (6 oz) redcurrants
4 tablespoons red wine
approx. 40 g (1½ oz) caster sugar
1 level teaspoon arrowroot

Preparation time: *30 minutes, plus setting time*

Put the eggs into a heatproof bowl. Add 50 g (2 oz) sugar and beat until creamy. Warm the milk slightly and whisk into the eggs. Strain into a heat-proof bowl and stand over a pan of very gently simmering water. Cook, stirring frequently until the custard thickens sufficiently to coat the back of the spoon quite thickly. Remove from the heat. Put the rum and the water into a heatproof basin with the gelatine. Stand over the simmering water until dissolved. Cool a little and then stir evenly through the custard, fol-lowed by the yogurt. Chill until beginning to thicken. Set aside 8 strawber-ries for decoration and slice the remainder. Pour the setting custard into 4–6 glasses alternating with sliced strawberries. Chill to set.

For the sauce: put the redcurrants and the wine into a saucepan and stew gently until soft. Add sugar to taste. Blend the arrowroot with the minimum of cold water, add to the sauce and cook gently until the mixture is clear. Cool. Either serve the mousses with a layer of sauce spooned over the top of each one and decorate with halved or quartered strawberries or serve the sauce separately using just strawberries for decoration.

Gooseberry Ice Cream

A delicately flavoured ice cream with a hint of orange which can be made from fresh or frozen gooseberries.

Serves 8

568 ml (1 pint) milk
1 vanilla pod
6 egg yolks
175 g (6 oz) caster sugar
225–350 g (8–12 oz) gooseberries,
*   topped and tailed*

sugar to taste
finely grated rind of ½ orange
568 ml (1 pint) double cream
julienne strips of orange rind to
decorate

Preparation time: *45 minutes, plus chilling and freezing time*

Bring the milk and vanilla pod almost to the boil, remove from the heat and leave to stand for up to 30 minutes. Discard the pod. Beat the egg yolks and sugar together, stir in the milk and strain back into the pan. Cook the custard very gently, either directly on the heat or over a pan of gently sim-mering water until it thickens sufficiently to coat the back of a spoon. Leave to cool. Stew the gooseberries in the minimum of water until tender – about 10 minutes, then sieve. Sweeten barely to taste, then stir evenly through the custard adding the orange rind. Pour into a shallow freezer container and when cold, freeze until mushy. Turn the mushy mixture into a cold bowl and whisk until quite smooth. Whip the cream and fold through the mixture. Return to the freezer until firm. Serve decorated with fine strips of orange rind. *Variation:* other fruits such as blackcurrants and peaches can be used instead, as can strawberries and raspberries which need only sieving not stewing.

Brown Bread Ice Cream

It sounds peculiar but it tastes delicious and is a real old–fashioned favourite.

Serves 6

*100 g (4 oz) wholemeal bread, crust
  removed*
450 ml (¾ pint) double cream
100 g (4 oz) icing sugar, sifted

½ teaspoon vanilla essence
50 g (2 oz) granulated sugar
50 ml (2 fl oz) water

Preparation time: *40 minutes plus chilling and freezing time*
Heat the oven to 140°C/275°F/Gas Mark 1.

Put the sliced bread in a slow oven for about an hour or until crisp and dry. Crush in a blender or food processor to make fine crumbs. Whip the cream until just standing in soft peaks and stir in the icing sugar and vanilla essence. Turn the mixture into an ice tray or shallow rigid container and freeze for an hour or until the cream is starting to freeze around the edges. Meanwhile, place the sugar and water in a small saucepan and stir over a low heat until the sugar dissolves. Increase the heat and boil for 2 minutes without stirring. Remove from the heat, stir in the breadcrumbs and leave until cold. As the ice cream begins to freeze, remove from the freezer and turn into a cold bowl. Beat until creamy, stir in the breadcrumbs and replace the mixture in the container. Freeze until hard.

Ice Cream Bombe

This makes an excellent alternative to a Christmas pudding; but can equally well be served at any other time of year.

Serves 8

3 eggs
568 ml (1 pint) milk
75 g (3 oz) caster sugar
1 level tablespoon powdered gelatine
2 tablespoons water
2–3 tablespoons brandy
*300 ml (½ pint) double or whipping
  cream*
25 g (1 oz) toasted hazelnuts, chopped

25 g (1 oz) glacé cherries, chopped
25 g (½ oz) angelica, finely chopped
*40 g (1½ oz) plain chocolate, coarsely
  grated*
25 g (1 oz) raisins, chopped (optional)

To Decorate:
whipped cream
glace cherries

Preparation time: *1 hour plus chilling and freezing time*

Whisk the eggs in a basin. Heat the milk to just below boiling point and whisk into the eggs with the sugar. Put the basin over a pan of gently simmering water (or use a double saucepan) and stir over a gentle heat until the custard begins to thicken; continue until it will coat the back of a spoon. Cool to lukewarm. Put the gelatine with the water into a small basin and when the water has been absorbed stand the basin in the hot water pan and heat until the gelatine is syrupy and clear. Cool a little and stir into the custard with the brandy. When the custard is cold whip the cream until it stands in soft peaks and fold evenly through the mixture. Cover the bowl and beat until smooth. Spread about ⅔ of the ice cream around the inside of a lightly greased 1.2 litre (2 pint) pudding basin and chill until firm; you may need to press it back round the sides of the basin as it firms up. Alternatively place a smaller basin inside to keep the shape.

Meanwhile, keep the remainder of the ice cream in the refrigerator; it must not melt or freeze too hard. Stir chopped nuts, cherries, angelica and chocolate into the ice cream with the raisins (if used) and spoon into the centre of the ice cream–lined basin. Level the top and freeze until firm – at least 24 hours. *To serve:* unmould the bombe on a plate and decorate with whipped cream and glacé cherries. Leave in the refrigerator to 'come to' for 15–20 minutes before serving.

Chocolate Soufflé

Everyone's favourite soufflé which can be flavoured with vanilla or rum to suit your taste.

Serves 8

6 eggs (size 2 or 3), separated
6 tablespoons of water
175 g (6 oz) caster sugar
175 g (6 oz) plain chocolate or chocolate dots
2 level tablespoons powdered gelatine
3 tablespoons rum
or 3 tablespoons of water flavoured with a few drops of vanilla essence

300 ml (½ pint) double or whipping cream

To decorate:
little grated chocolate or crushed ratafia biscuits
8 natural glacé cherries or maraschino cherries

Preparation time: *45 minutes, plus chilling time*

Prepare a 15 cm (6 inch) (approx. 1.2 litre/2 pint) soufflé dish by tying a double thickness band of greased greaseproof paper around the sides of a 600 ml (1 pint) soufflé dish so the paper comes about 5 cm (2 inches) above the top of the dish. Put the egg yolks in a large heatproof bowl with 4 table-spoons water and the sugar. Whisk over a pan of gently simmering water until thick, pale in colour and the whisk leaves a heavy trail when lifted. Remove from the heat and beat until cool. Melt the chocolate in a heatproof basin over the simmering water, and stir until smooth. Dissolve the gelatine in a basin with the remaining water and rum, or water and vanilla essence. Stir first the chocolate and then the dissolved gelatine into the whisked mixture until evenly blended. Leave until beginning to thicken.

Whip the cream until thick and floppy and then fold quickly and evenly through the mixture. Finally whisk the egg whites stiffly and fold through the mixture. Pour quickly into the prepared dish and chill until set. *To serve:* peel off the paper collar and use the grated chocolate or ratafia biscuit crumbs to coat the sides of the soufflé. Whip the reserved cream until thick and use to pipe 8 whirls on top of the soufflé. Top each with a cherry.

Burnt Cream or Crème Brulée

A traditional favourite devised by Trinity College, Cambridge. An ideal dish to serve as it is or with fresh fruit or fruit salads.

Serves 8

2 eggs
4 egg yolks 50 g
(2 oz) caster sugar
½ teaspoon vanilla essence

568 ml (1 pint) single or whipping
  cream
150 ml (¼ pint) single cream or milk

Topping:
caster sugar

Preparation time: *15 minutes*
Cooking time: *1¼ hours*
Heat the oven to 150°C/300°F/Gas Mark 2.

Beat the eggs, egg yolks and sugar together then whisk in the vanilla essence, cream and milk. Strain into a shallow ovenproof dish and stand in a roasting tin with water coming half-way up the sides of the dish. Cook in a cool oven for about an hour or until set and a knife inserted in the centre comes out clean. Cool, then chill thoroughly. Spoon an even layer of caster sugar over the surface of the custard about 5 mm (¼ inch) thick. Put under a preheated moderate grill and cook until the sugar melts and turns an even caramel colour all over – turning the dish as necessary. Cool and chill again before serving. *To serve:* tap the caramel with the back of a spoon to break it up.

Note: this can be made 24 hours in advance.

Hazelnut and Peach Cheesecake

Cheesecakes are great favourites and this one has an interesting 'crunch' given by the hazelnuts.

Serves 8

65 g (2½ oz) butter or margarine
100 g (4 oz) digestive biscuits, crushed
25 g (1 oz) toasted chopped hazelnuts

Cheesecake:
15 g (½ oz) packet powdered gelatine
75 g (3 oz) caster sugar

150 ml (¼ pint) milk
2 eggs (size 2 or 3), separated
225 g (8 oz) full fat soft cheese
150 ml (¼ pint) soured cream
grated rind and juice of 1 large lemon

Topping:
24 toasted hazelnuts
100 g (4 oz) caster sugar
1 tablespoon water
2 fresh peaches or a small can of sliced
    peaches, drained
25 g (1 oz) butter
25 g (1 oz) caster sugar

Preparation time: 45 minutes, plus chilling time

For the base: melt the butter and stir in the biscuit crumbs and hazelnuts. Press into the base of a well greased 18–20 cm (7–8 inch) loose–based cake tin or deep flan ring and chill until set. *For the cheesecake:* put the gelatine into a saucepan with sugar and milk and heat very gently without boiling, until the gelatine is completely dissolved. Remove from the heat, beat in the egg yolks and leave until cool. Soften the cheese and beat in the soured cream and lemon rind and juice until smooth, then gradually beat in the gelatine mixture. Leave until on the point of setting then whisk the egg white stiffly and fold through the mixture. Pour over the base and chill until set. *To caramelize the hazelnuts:* rub off skins and place in clusters of three on a well greased baking sheet. Put sugar and water into a pan, heat gently until dissolved then boil until a caramel colour. Quickly pour or spoon a little over each cluster and leave to set. *To serve:* remove the cheesecake from the tin and arrange the hazelnut clusters around the top edge. Slice the peaches and dip in a mixture of butter melted with the sugar to glaze; then arrange in the centre of the cheesecake. Serve in slices.

Paris Brest de Pommes

A large choux pastry ring which is split and filled with a type of frangipane cream and poached apples; makes a real dinner party dessert.

Serves 6

50 g (2 oz) butter
150 ml (¼ pint) water
65 g (2½ oz) plain flour
pinch of salt
2 eggs (size 2), beaten
about 15 g (½ oz) flaked or chopped
    almonds

Crème Frangipane:
2 egg yolks
50 g (2 oz) caster sugar
30 g (1¼ oz) cornflour

300 ml (½ pint) milk
almond essence
25 g (1 oz) butter
50 g (2 oz) ground almonds

Filling:
450 g (1 lb) cooking apples
2 tablespoons lemon juice
grated rind of 1 lemon
about 6 level tablespoons caster sugar
150 ml (¼ pint) whipping cream
icing sugar to decorate

Preparation time: *1 hour*
Cooking time: *25–30 minutes*
Heat the oven to 220°C/425°F/Gas Mark 7.

For the pastry: put the butter and water into a saucepan and heat gently until the fat melts. Bring quickly to the boil then sift in the flour and salt all at once and beat quickly to form a smooth ball of paste. Remove from the heat, spread out over the base of the pan and leave to cool to lukewarm. Using a hand–held electric mixer for preference, gradually beat in the beaten egg a little at a time (reserving 1 teaspoon for glazing) until the mixture becomes smooth and glossy and holds its shape. Pipe or spread into a ring about 20 cm (8 inches) in diameter on a greased baking sheet. Brush with the reserved egg and sprinkle with almonds. Bake in a hot oven for 20 minutes. Reduce the temperature to moderately hot (190°C/ 375°F/Gas Mark 5) and continue for about 25 minutes or until well risen, golden brown and firm to the touch. Remove to a wire rack and make horizontal slits in the side of the ring to allow the steam to escape. Leave to cool.

For the Crème Frangipane: Beat the egg yolks, sugar, cornflour and a little of the milk together in a bowl until smooth. Heat the remaining milk in a saucepan, pour on the egg mixture, return to the pan and bring to the boil, stirring continuously, until very thick and smooth. Remove from the heat and beat in a few drops of almond essence, butter and almonds. Cover and leave until cold. *For the filling:* Peel, core and slice the apples and put into a saucepan with the lemon juice, rind and just the minimum of water. Poach gently until the fruit is barely tender. Add caster sugar to taste, cover, and leave until cold.

To assemble: cut the choux ring in half horizontally and put the base on a serving plate. Whip the cream until thick and fold through the frangipane crème, then spread this into the base of the choux ring. Drain the apple slices and arrange on top of the filling. Replace the lid and dredge the top with icing sugar. Chill for up to 1 hour before serving.

Chocolate Chestnut Gâteau

This gâteau may be made the day before required. The chocolate flavoured sponge may be replaced with a vanilla or orange cake if preferred.

Serves 8

3 eggs (size 1 or 2)
115 g (4 ½ oz) caster sugar
75 g (3 oz) plain flour
20 g (¾ oz) cocoa powder

Filling:
425 g (15 oz) can unsweetened chestnut purée
2 tablespoons clear honey

300 ml (½ pint) double or whipping cream
3–4 tablespoons rum
100 g (4 oz) plain chocolate
2–4 marron glacé quartered or 8–10 glacé cherries
few chocolate matchsticks

Preparation time: *45 minutes*
Cooking time: *30 minutes*
Heat the oven to 190°C/375°F/Gas Mark 5.

For the cake: Line a tin 28 x 18 x 4 cm (11 x 7 x 1½ inches) with greased greaseproof or non–stick baking paper. Whisk the eggs and sugar together in a heatproof bowl over a pan of hot water until very pale and thick and the whisk leaves a heavy trail; remove from the heat. If using a large electric beater, no heat is necesary. Sift the flour and cocoa together twice and fold quickly and evenly through the whisked mixture. Turn into the prepared tin making sure there is sufficient mixture in the corners, and bake in a moderately hot oven for about 30 minutes or until well risen and firm to the touch. Turn out on to a wire rack and leave until cold.

For the filling: beat the chestnut purée until smooth then beat in the honey. Put about a quarter of the purée into a piping bag fitted with a large star vegetable nozzle and set aside. Whip cream until stiff and fold a quarter into the remaining chestnut mixture. Cut the cake in half lengthwise and sprinkle each half with rum. Sandwich together with the chestnut mixture. Use remaining cream to mask the whole cake. Using a potato peeler (or coarse grater) pare the chocolate into mini curls and use to coat the sides of the gâteau. Pipe a zig–zag of chestnut purée along the top of the gâteau and complete decoration with pieces of marron glacé or glacé cherries and chocolate matchsticks. Leave to stand for 3–4 hours before serving.

Chocolate Curls – melt about 100 g (4 oz) chocolate and spread it out thinly on a cold flat surface like formica or marble. Leave to set but not become too hard. Take a large sharp knife and keeping the blade at an angle of 45° gently push the knife away from you or pull it towards you shaving off a curl of chocolate. Don't cut too deeply or the curls will not form. Put on a plate and chill. Store in an airtight container between layers of waxed paper.

Chocolate leaves – melt about 50 g (2 oz) chocolate. Select perfect samples of small rose leaves or others which have strong veins on the underside. Make sure they are perfectly clean and dry. Using a small paint brush, brush the underside of the leaves with chocolate and put to dry in the refrigerator. When set, a second layer can be added. Chill until quite set and store in an airtight container for up to 2 weeks. Carefully peel off the leaf from the chocolate when required.

Freezing recommended: *for up to 1 month*

TEATIME

INTRODUCTION

Everyone enjoys a real home-made tea. The concept of 'tea' being more than just a cup of tea was introduced when people found they could not survive without hunger pangs from lunchtime to dinner time, so sweet-meats were offered mid–afternoon to quell these feelings. The idea caught on fast and was soon to include sandwiches, scones and a variety of buns and cakes – almost enough to make a full blown meal in itself rather than the 'hunger–pang stopper' it was supposed to be. Tea dances were intro-duced and became popular in the war years and in some places are being revived now; college students toast crumpets and teacakes in front of their gas fires to keep them going whilst studying; cream teas are a great favourite with holiday makers; and hotels serve a full set tea containing many mouthwatering delicacies.

Sandwiches with traditional fillings such as cucumber, egg and cress or ham can be served in small triangles or even more attractively as pinwheels. Scones come in a wide variety of flavours, shapes and textures; some baked in the oven, others cooked on griddles or bakestones, to serve with butter and possibly jam or honey. Crumpets or pikelets are readily available to toast and serve dripping with butter. Biscuits and cookies appear in numer-ous forms. Specialities such as brandy snaps and tuiles, oozing with cream, and many others are there to make your mouth water and are difficult to refuse. Finally come the teabreads and cakes too numerous to mention, ranging from plain to extremely fancy with cream, butter cream and other icings, some conservatively decorated and others so lavishly embellished that it is difficult to know how or where to make the first cut.

Whatever your fancy, teatime is here to tempt you into eating something mid–afternoon. Make and bake to suit your tastes and occasions but remember that some of the recipes should be made in advance, whilst others are at their best baked just before serving.

Hazelnut or Almond Tuiles

These can be shaped as curls or cornets and the flavouring of nuts chosen to suit your taste.

Makes about 15

1 egg white 50 g
(2 oz) caster sugar
25 g (1 oz) plain flour

25 g (1 oz) hazelnuts, skinned and very
finely chopped
or 25 g (1 oz) flaked almonds, chopped
25 g (1 oz) butter, melted and cooled

Preparation time: 20 minutes
Cooking time: 45 minutes
Heat the oven to 190°C/375°F/Gas Mark 5.

Line two baking sheets with non–stick baking paper. Lightly grease several thick wooden spoon handles or large cream horn tins. Whisk the egg white until very stiff and standing in peaks. Fold in the sugar, sifted flour and nuts and mix in evenly; finally fold in the butter. Place teaspoons of the mixture well apart on the baking sheets no more than 4 at a time, and spread out thinly. Bake in a moderately hot oven for 8–12 minutes or until browned just around the edge and golden in the centre. Cool only very slightly on the baking sheets, then remove quickly and curl around the handles. Leave until firm, then slide off and put onto wire racks. For cream horn tins, wind quickly around the tins, pressing firmly into place or if necessary slipping the covered tin into another tin to hold it in place as it cools. Store in an airtight container for up to 10 days.

Honey Cinnamon Buns

Sponge buns flavoured with honey and sandwiched together with raspberry jam.

50 g (2 oz) butter
50 g (2 oz) whipped white fat
75 g (3 oz) soft brown sugar
1 egg (size 1 or 2), beaten
2 tablespoons clear honey

175 g (7 oz) plain flour
½ level teaspoon bicarbonate of soda
½ level teaspoon ground cinnamon
raspberry jam or thick honey
icing sugar for decoration

Preparation time: 20 minutes, plus chilling time
Cooking time: 25 minutes
Heat the oven to 180°C/350°F/Gas Mark 4.

Grease 2 baking sheets. Cream the fats together until well blended then add the sugar and continue to beat until very light and fluffy. Beat in the egg thoroughly, followed by honey. Sift the flour, bicarbonate of soda and cinnamon together and work into the mixture. Cover and chill until firm.

Roll the dough into balls about the size of a walnut and place well apart on the baking sheet. Bake in a moderate oven for about 12 minutes or until well risen and lightly coloured. Remove carefully to a wire rack and leave to cool. When cold sandwich together with raspberry jam or clear honey and just before serving dredge lightly with icing sugar.

Brandy Snaps

Everyone's favourite for teatime or to eat as a dessert filled with cream.

Makes approx. 12 snaps or cornets

50 g (2 oz) butter or margarine　　　*50 g (2 oz) plain flour*
50 g (2 oz) golden syrup　　　*½ level teaspoon ground ginger*
50 g (2 oz) caster sugar

Preparation time: *25 minutes*
Cooking time: *1 hour*
Heat the oven to 160°C/325°F/Gas Mark 3.

Line 2 or 3 baking sheets with non–stick baking paper. For snaps grease several wooden spoon handles; or for cornets grease several cream horn tins. Place the butter, syrup and sugar into a saucepan and heat gently until melted. Remove from the heat. Sift the flour and ginger together and stir evenly into the mixture. Place 3 or 4 teaspoons of the mixture on the baking sheets and spread out a little. Keep fairly well apart as they do spread during cooking. Bake in a very moderate oven for 10–15 minutes until golden brown. Leave until beginning to firm up a little then quickly wind round the spoon handles for the snaps or the cream horn tins for the cornets. Place on a wire rack to cool and crisp up and then remove from the handles or tins. Repeat with the rest of the mixture. They will store satisfactorily for 3–4 weeks in an airtight container.

Fruited Flapjacks

A variation on an old favourite, which makes them even moreish.

Makes 9–12 pieces

100 g (4 oz) butter or margarine　　　*50 g (2 oz) raisins*
50 g (2 oz) natural demerara sugar　　　*25 g (1 oz) dried apricots, chopped*
2 tablespoons thick honey　　　*25 g (1 oz) shelled pecans or walnuts,*
¾ level teaspoon mixed spice, ground　　　 *coarsely chopped*
* cinnamon or ground ginger*　　　*200 g (7 oz) rolled oats*

Preparation time: *15 minutes*
Cooking time: *40 minutes*
Heat the oven to 180°C/350°F/Gas Mark 4.

Melt the fat in a pan with the sugar and honey. Add the spice and then the dried fruits followed by the nuts and oats. Mix thoroughly and press the mixture into a well greased shallow 20 cm (8 inch) square tin. Cook in a moderate oven for about 40 minutes until firm. Mark deeply into square or triangles but leave until cold before cutting and removing from the tin. Store in an airtight container.

Scones

This is my special recipe for scones; there are many others to choose from as most people have their own particular favourite.

Makes 8–10 scones

225 g (8 oz) self raising flour
pinch salt
50 g (2 oz) butter or margarine
1 level tablespoon caster sugar
   (optional)

1 egg (size 2 or 3), beaten
about 5 tablespoons milk or soured milk
beaten egg or milk to glaze

Preparation time: *10 minutes*
Cooking time: *15 minutes*
Heat the oven to 230°C/450°F/Gas Mark 8.

Either grease a baking sheet or dredge it liberally with flour. Sift the flour and salt into a bowl. Add the fat and rub in until the mixture resembles fine breadcrumbs. Stir in the sugar, if used. Add the egg and sufficient milk to mix to a fairly soft dough using a palette knife or spatula. Turn out onto a lightly floured surface and gently flatten the dough out to about 2 – 2.5 cm (¾ to 1 inch) thick. Using a well floured plain or fluted cutter of about 4–5 cm (1½–2 inches) or an upturned glass, stamp out the scones. Reroll trimmings to cut out more scones. Place on the baking sheet and either brush the tops with beaten egg or milk or dredge lightly with flour. Bake in a hot oven for 12–15 minutes until well risen, golden brown and just firm. Remove to a wire rack and leave to cool. Scones are best eaten the day they are made, but they reheat well and freeze for up to 3 months.

Variations: **Fruit** – add 50 g (2 oz) currants, sultanas, raisins or cut mixed peel to the dried ingredients.
   Cheese – omit the sugar and add a pinch of dried mustard and 40–50 g (1½–2 oz) finely grated mature Cheddar cheese; or 1–2 level tablespoons grated Parmesan cheese to the dried ingredients.

Welsh Cakes

A traditional rich fruited griddle cake found all over Wales but more often in the South. These are rolled thicker than some of the griddle scones and cakes and are rather larger than most. Eat whilst really fresh with plenty of butter.

Makes about 12

225 g (8 oz) plain flour
pinch of salt
1 level teaspoon baking powder
good pinch each mixed spice and
    ground nutmeg
125 g (5 oz) butter or margarine

75 g (3 oz) caster sugar
40 g (1½ oz) currants
40 g (1½ oz) sultanas
1 egg (size 2 or 3), beaten
approx. 2 tablespoons milk

Preparation time: 15 minutes
Cooking time: 20 minutes

Sift the flour, salt and baking powder and spices into a bowl and rub in the fat. Mix in the sugar, currants, sultanas and then add the egg and sufficient milk to mix to a pliable dough, similar to shortcrust pastry. Turn onto a floured surface and roll out to about 1 cm (½ inch) thick. Cut into plain or fluted 7.5 cm (3 inch) rounds. Cook on a moderately heated, greased griddle, heavy–based frying pan or bakestone for about 3–4 minutes each side or until golden brown. If cooked too quickly they will burn on the outside and still be soggy inside. Serve plain or dredged with sugar or a mixture of cinnamon and sugar; either warm or cold with butter.

Pinwheel Sandwiches

An attractive and practical way to serve sandwiches for a party. Make them the day before to make sure they hold together, then simply cut into slices when required. Each filling is sufficient for one large loaf.

Each roll should give 8–12 slices, making a total of 80–120 pinwheels per loaf.

1 large white or brown tin loaf, uncut
and chilled for ease of cutting
approx. 175 g (6 oz) butter or other
spread

Crab and Gherkin Filling:
2–3 large jars of crabpaste
jar of midget gherkins

Egg and Cress Filling:
6 hard–boiled eggs

3–4 tablespoons mayonnaise
salt and pepper to taste
3 cartons mustard and cress, chopped

Pâté and Olive Filling:
225 g (8 oz) smooth pâté
a little natural yogurt or soured cream
salt, pepper and garlic to taste
jar of stuffed green olives

Preparation time: 1 hour, plus chilling time

Cut off the crust all round the loaf, then spread one long side lightly with butter. Cut off a slice about 1 cm (⅜ inch) thick, keeping it even. Repeat the spreading and slicing right across the loaf – you should get about 10 slices.

For Crab and Gherkin Pinwheels: spread each slice with crab paste then arrange a line of drained midget gherkins along one short edge. Roll up tightly, beginning at the edge with the gherkins, then wrap at once in cling–film and refrigerate until required.

For Egg and Cress Pinwheels: mash the hard–boiled eggs finely, adding the mayonnaise, salt and pepper to taste and the chopped mustard and cress. Spread each slice with this mixture, then roll up, wrap in cling–film and refrigerate as before.

For Pâté and Olive Pinwheels: beat the pâté until smooth, adding a little yogurt or sour cream, if necessary to give a good spreading consistency. Season with salt, pepper and garlic to taste. Spread each slice with this mixture then arrange a line of well–drained stuffed olives along one short edge. Roll up, wrap in cling–film and refrigerate as above.

To Serve: remove the cling–film and cut the rolls into pinwheel slices.

Courgette and Tarragon Quiches

Good for teatime but also to put in packed lunches or to serve at cocktail parties.

Makes 30–36

Pastry:
225 g (8 oz) plain or granary flour
pinch of salt 50 g (2 oz) butter or block
*   margarine 50 g (2 oz) lard or white*
*   fat*
cold water to mix

Filling:
2 courgettes (approx. 175 g (6 oz))
4 spring onions, trimmed and chopped
or 2 level tablespoons finely chopped

onion
1 level tablespoon freshly chopped
tarragon
*   or 2 level teaspoons dried tarragon*
2 eggs (size 2 or 3)
150 ml (¼ pint) double or soured cream
4 tablespoons milk
salt and pepper

Preparation time: *25 minutes*
Cooking time: *25 minutes*
Heat the oven to 200°C/400°F/Gas Mark 6.

Make up the shortcrust pastry (see page 26), wrap in polythene and chill until required. Top and tail the courgettes then grate coarsely into a bowl. Cover liberally with boiling water, mixed well, then leave to stand for 10 minutes. Drain very thoroughly, pressing out the excess water with a potato masher. Mix with the onion and tarragon. Beat the eggs, cream, milk and seasonings together. Roll out the pastry, cut out fluted circles of approx 8 cm (3½ inches) in diameter and use to line 30–36 patty tins. Divide the courgette mixture between them then add the egg custard (they should be almost full). Cook in a fairly hot oven for aboout 25 minutes until set and lightly brown. Cool on a wire rack.

Freezing recommended: *for up to 2 months.*

Sausage and Salami Rolls

As a change from the normal filling, these have a mixture of sausagemeat and salami.

Makes between 15 and 25

350 g (12 oz) pork or beef sausagemeat
100 g (4 oz) salami, minced or finely
  chopped
black pepper

350 g (12 oz) ready made puff pastry
beaten egg or top of the milk to glaze
sesame seeds

Preparation time: 30 minutes
Cooking time: 25 minutes
Heat the oven to 220°C/425°F/Gas Mark 7.

Combine the sausagemeat and salami and season with black pepper. Roll out the pastry thinly and cut into strips approx. 10 cm (4 inches) wide. Form the sausagemeat into rolls about 2.5 cm (1 inch) in diameter and lay along the centre of the pastry strips. Damp the edges of the pastry with water, fold over and press firmly together. Flake the edges with a knife and then cut into 4, 5 or 6 cm (1½, 2 or 2½ inch) lengths. Brush with beaten egg or milk and make 2 or 3 cuts in the top of each one. Sprinkle with sesame seeds and place on dampened baking sheets. Cook in a hot oven for 20–25 minutes, depending on size, until well browned and crisp. Cool on wire racks. Store in a refrigerator for up to 2 days.

Freezing recommended: for up to 1 month

Hazelnut Florentines

Richly fruited wafers backed with chocolate.

Makes 24–30

75 g (3 oz) butter
100 g (4 oz) caster sugar
100 g (4 oz) hazelnuts, skinned and
  chopped
25 g (1 oz) raisins, chopped
25 g (1 oz) chopped mixed peel

40 g (1½ oz) glacé cherries
40 g (1½ oz) dried apricots, chopped
  (preferably the 'no–need–to–soak'
  variety)
finely grated rind of ½ orange
175 g (6 oz) plain chocolate

Preparation time: 30 minutes
Cooking time: 1 hour
Heat the oven to 180°C/350°F/Gas Mark 4.

Line two or three baking sheets with non–stick paper. Melt the butter and sugar in a saucepan and boil for one minute. Remove from the heat and stir in all the remaining ingredients except the chocolate. Leave to cool. Put teaspoons of the mixture well apart on the baking sheet – only 4 or 5 per sheet. Bake in the centre of a moderate oven for 10–12 minutes or until golden brown. Cool until just firm, pressing the edges back to a neat shape. Remove carefully to a wire rack and leave until cold and firm. Store for up to a week in an airtight container with sheets of non–stick paper between them before adding the chocolate. A day or so before required, melt the chocolate and spread a little over the smooth side of each florentine. As it sets, mark into wavy lines with a fork, then leave to harden.

Orange and Cardamom Biscuits

Crisp biscuits with just a hint of spiciness.

Makes about 25

125 g (5 oz) plain flour
25 g (1 oz) ground rice
10 cardamom seeds
grated rind of 1 orange
100 g (4 oz) butter or margarine
50 g (2 oz) light soft brown sugar

Icing (optional):
75 g (3 oz) butter
100 g (4 oz) icing sugar, sifted
few drops orange flower water
few drops orange colouring (optional)
orange jelly slices

Preparation time: *25 minutes*
Cooking time: *30 minutes*
Heat the oven 180°C/350°F/Gas Mark 4.

Sift the flour and ground rice into a bowl. Remove the seeds from the cardamom pods and crush thoroughly, then add to the dry ingredients with the orange rind, butter and sugar. Work together until the mixture is smooth and pliable then roll out to about 5 mm (¼ inch) thick. Cut into 7.5 cm (3 inch) fluted rounds and place on greased baking sheets. Prick 2 or 3 times with a fork and then cook in a moderate oven for about 25 minutes until lightly browned. Cool on a wire rack and store in an airtight container until required. *To serve iced:* cream the butter with the sugar until soft and beat in orange flower water and colouring, if liked. Put into a piping bag with a star nozzle and pipe an 's' shape on to each biscuit; decorate with an orange jelly slice.

Lime Creams

Light textured crisp biscuits flavoured with lime and sandwiched together with a tangy lime butter cream.

Makes about 12

100 g (4 oz) butter or margarine
100 g (4 oz) caster sugar
2 teaspoons golden syrup

finely grated rind of 1 lime
1 egg yolk
150 g (6 oz) plain flour

25 g (1 oz) custard powder
½ level teaspoon cream of tartar
½ level teaspoon bicarbonate of soda

Filling:
40 g (1½ oz) butter
75 g (3 oz) icing sugar, sifted
little grated lime rind
approx. 1 teaspoon lime juice

Preparation time: 30 minutes
Cooking time: 20 minutes
Heat the oven to 190°C/375°F/Gas Mark 5.

Grease two or three baking sheets or cover with non–stick baking paper. Cream the fat and sugar together until very light and fluffy. Beat in the syrup, lime rind and egg yolk. Sift the flour, custard powder, cream of tartar and bicarbonate of soda together and work into the creamed mixture. Roll into balls the size of a small walnut and arrange on the baking sheet allowing plenty of room for them to spread. Bake in a moderately hot oven for about 20 minutes until golden brown. Remove carefully to a wire rack and leave to cool. *For the filling:* cream the butter and sugar together, then beat in the lime rind and sufficient lime juice to give a thick spreading consistency. Use to sandwich the biscuits together. Do not assemble more than a few hours before required.

Danish Pastries

These soft–textured favourites, filled with marzipan and decorated with glacé icing, nuts and glacé cherries, will disappear almost as soon as they are made.

Makes about 24

25 g (1 oz) fresh yeast
  or 1 level tablespoon dried yeast and
  1 level teaspoon caster sugar
150 ml (¼ pint) warm water
450 g (1 lb) plain flour (not strong
  flour)
pinch of salt
50 g (2 oz) lard or white fat
25 g (1 oz) caster sugar
2 eggs (size 2 or 3) beaten
275 g (10 oz) butter

175 g (6 oz) marzipan
beaten egg to glaze

Glacé Icing:
225 g (8 oz) icing sugar, sifted
lemon juice

Topping:
chopped toasted hazelnuts or almonds
angelica strips
glacé cherries

Preparation time: 1 hour, plus rising time
Cooking time: 1 hour

Blend the fresh yeast with the water; if using dried yeast, dissolve the sugar in the water, sprinkle on top and leave in a warm place for about 10 minutes until frothy. Sift the flour and salt in a bowl, rub in the fat and mix in the sugar. Add the yeast liquid and beaten eggs to the dry ingredients and mix to form a soft and elastic dough, adding a little more water if necessary. Turn onto a lightly floured surface and knead by hand until smooth – about 2–3 minutes. Put into an oiled polythene bag chill in the refrigerator for 10 minutes.

Soften the butter until it can be shaped into an oblong approx 23 x 10 cm (19 x 4 inches). Remove the dough and roll it out to a 28 cm (11 inch) square. Spread the butter down the centre of it. Enclose the butter by folding the flaps of dough to overlap in the middle. Seal the top and bottom with a rolling pin, then roll out to a strip three times as long as it is wide. Fold the bottom third upwards and the top third downwards and seal the edges. Return to the polythene bag and chill for 10 minutes. Repeat the rolling, folding and resting three more times, giving the pastry a quarter turn each time so that the fold is at the side. Chill for 30 minutes. The dough is then ready to shape.

Heat the oven to 220°C/425°F/Gas Mark 7. Using half the dough, roll out thinly and cut into squares of 7.5 cm (3 inches) or a little larger if preferred. Make diagonal cuts from each corner to within 2.5 cm (1 inch) of the centre. Place a ball of marzipan in the centre of each square and then fold each corner of the square to the centre, securing the tips with water or beaten egg. Cover lightly with an oiled sheet of polythene and put to rise in a warm place for about 20 minutes until well risen and puffy. Roll out half the remaining dough and trim to a circle of approx 25 cm (10 inches) then cut into 6 even–sized wedges. Put a roll of marzipan at the thick end of the dough and roll up from the wide base to the tip to enclose the filling. Bend to a crescent and glaze, then prove as for the windmills. Repeat with the remaining dough. Bake in a hot oven allowing 15–20 minutes for both shapes, until they are a good golden brown colour and crisp. Cool on wire racks.

To decorate: blend the icing sugar with sufficient lemon juice to give an icing that will coat the back of a spoon quite thickly. Spread a little over each of the pastries, sprinkle immediately with a few coated nuts and decorate with pieces of angelica and glacé cherry. Leave to set.

Chocolate Brownies

An American favourite – these are chewy nut and chocolate squares with a crisp and crumbly top.

Makes 12–16

50 g (2 oz) plain chocolate
65 g (2½ oz) butter or margarine
150 g (6 oz) caster sugar
½ teaspoon vanilla essence
65 g (2½ oz) self raising flour

pinch of salt
50 g (2 oz) walnuts, chopped
2 eggs, beaten
icing sugar to decorate

Preparation time: *20 minutes*
Cooking time: *40 minutes*
Heat the oven to 180°C/350°F/Gas Mark 4.

Grease and flour a shallow 20 cm (8 inch) square cake tin; or line with greased greaseproof or non–stick baking paper. Put the broken up chocolate into a bowl with the the butter and stand over a pan of gently simmering water. Stir until melted, then beat in the sugar and essence. Alternatively melt in a microwave oven on Maximum/100% for about 2 minutes. Remove from the heat. Sift the flour and salt into a bowl and add the walnuts. Add the eggs and chocolate mixture, beat well until smooth and then pour into the prepared tin. Bake in a moderate oven for 35–40 minutes or until well risen and just beginning to shrink away from the sides of the tin. Cool in the tin and when cold cut into 12 squares or fingers. Sprinkle with sifted icing sugar before serving. Store in an airtight container for up to 2 weeks.

Blueberry and Apple Strudels

If you can find fresh blueberries, they can be used raw; otherwise use frozen ones. Simply mix the blueberries with the apples and sugar.

Makes 8

*1 recipe quantity strudel pastry (see
   page 87)
or 8 sheets of phyllo pastry*

Filling:
*225 g (8 oz) frozen blueberries, thawed
75 g (3 oz) caster sugar*

*¼ level teaspoon ground allspice
450 g (1 lb) cooking apples, peeled,
   cored and diced
75 g (3 oz) butter, melted
icing sugar for dredging*

Preparation time: *1 hour, plus resting time*
Cooking time: *30 minutes*
Heat the oven to 190°C/375°F/Gas Mark 5.

Make up the strudel pastry as for Apple Strudels (on page 87). Drain off the excess juice from the thawed blueberries and mix in the sugar, spice and apples. Prepare the pastry by rolling out and pulling as for the Apple Strudel and cut into 8 even–sized pieces; or lay out the sheets of phyllo pastry, four at a time. Brush with melted butter, then place equal amounts of filling at the bottom of each piece leaving a margin all round. Fold over the margins and roll up carefully, making sure there are no tears and that the edges are all folded well in; otherwise the filling will seep out. Place on a greased baking sheet and brush with melted butter. Cook in a moderate oven for about 30 minutes until golden brown. Serve hot, or warm, lightly dredged with sifted icing sugar.

Ginger Meringues

A light brown meringue made with soft brown sugar to give a lively gooey centre and flavouring of ginger, which may be omitted, if preferred.

Makes 12–16 meringues filled with cream

75 g (3 oz) caster sugar
75 g (3 oz) light soft brown sugar
1 level teaspoon ground ginger
3 egg whites

Filling:
150 ml (¼ pint) double cream
1 tablespoon milk
3–4 pieces stem ginger or crystallized ginger, chopped

Preparation time: 25 minutes
Cooking time: 2 hours
Heat the oven to 150°C/300°F/Gas Mark 2.

Sift the sugars together with the ginger. Whisk the egg whites until very stiff and dry and standing in peaks. Whisk in the sugar mixture a tablespoon at a time making sure the meringue is stiff again before adding further sugar. Place in a piping bag fitted with a large star vegetable nozzle. Cover two baking sheets with non–stick baking paper and pipe whirls or batons of meringue on to the paper. Cook in a cool oven for about 2 hours, reversing the trays in the oven after an hour. The meringues should peel off the paper easily when ready. Cool on a wire rack and store in an airtight container until required. *To serve:* whip the cream and milk together, chop the ginger, sprinkle over the cream and use to sandwich the meringues together. Serve within 2 hours of assembling, if possible. They may also be served plain.

Spiced Whisky Cake

An unusual type of sponge cake, very moist and delicious but a little difficult to handle.

200 g (8 oz) sultanas
150 ml (¼ pint) water
100 g (4 oz) butter or margarine
125 g (5 oz) soft light brown sugar
1 egg (size 1 or 2), beaten
150 g (6 oz) plain flour
1 level teaspoon bicarbonate of soda
½ level teaspoon grated or ground nutmeg
¼ level teaspoon ground cinnamon

75 g (3 oz) walnuts or pecan nuts, chopped
2 tablespoons whisky

Butter Cream:
75 g (3 oz) butter
1 egg yolk
200 g (8 oz) icing sugar, sifted
1 tablespoon whisky
walnut halves or pecan halves for decoration

Preparation time: 30 minutes
Cooking time: 40 minutes
Heat the oven to 180°C/350°F/Gas Mark 4.

110

Grease two 20 cm (8 inch) round deep sandwich tins and line the base with greased greaseproof or non–stick paper. Put the sultanas and water into a small pan and bring to the boil. Simmer gently for 15 minutes then strain off the liquor and make up to 100 ml (4 fl oz) with cold water. Leave to cool. Cream the butter or margarine and sugar together until very pale and fluffy, then beat in the egg. Sift the flour with the soda and spices and fold into the mixture alternating wth the sultana liquor. Add the walnuts, sultanas and the whisky, and mix lightly but evenly. Divide between the tins and level the tops. Bake in a moderate oven for 30–35 minutes or until firm. Cool for a few minutes in the tin, then loosen the edges and turn out very carefully on to a wire rack to cool.

For the butter cream: melt the butter in a saucepan, remove from the heat and beat in the egg yolk. Gradually beat in the icing sugar alternating with the whisky, until light, smooth and fluffy. Use about ⅓ to sandwich the cake together and the remainder to spread over the top. Make an attractive design on the top using a round–bladed knife and decorate with walnuts or pecans.

Christmas Cake

This cake is flavoured with sherry before cooking, but you can improve it even more by pouring sherry or brandy over it at weekly intervals whilst it is maturing.

300 g (11 oz) currants
300 g (11 oz) sultanas
225 g (8 oz) raisins
75 g (3 oz) cut mixed peel
50 g (2 oz) ground almonds
150 g (5 oz) glacé cherries, quartered,
  washed and dried
grated rind of 1 orange
grated rind of 1 lemon
200 g (7 oz) butter
200 g (7 oz) dark soft brown or
  muscovado sugar

4 eggs (size 1 or 2)
1 tablespoon black treacle
1 teaspoon gravy browning (optional)
  65 g (2½ oz) self–raising flour
175 g (6 oz) plain flour
1 level teaspoon ground cinnamon
¾ level teaspoon mixed spice
good pinch of ground allspice
3 tablespoons sherry
sherry or brandy to pour over the cake
  (optional)

Preparation time: *1 hour*
Cooking time: *3¼ hours*
Heat the oven to 150°C/300°F/Gas Mark 2.

Grease and line a 20 cm (8 inch) round cake tin with double greased grease-proof paper. Combine the dried fruits, peel, almonds, cherries and fruit rinds. Cream the butter until light and fluffy then add the sugar and con-tinue to cream until light and fluffy and pale in colour. Beat in the eggs, one at a time, with the treacle and gravy browning (if used), following each one with a spoonful of flour. Sift the remaining flours with the spices and work into the mixture. Fold in the fruits followed by the sherry. Turn into the prepared tin and level the top. Tie several thicknesses of newspaper around the outside of the tin and cook in a cool oven for about 3¼ hours or until firm to touch and when a skewer is inserted in the centre it comes out clean.

Cool in the tin. Remove and wrap in foil. At weekly intervals prick the surface of the cake and pour 2–3 tablespoons sherry over it before rewrapping.

Apple and Spice Cake

This moist fruit cake is also good made with ripe pears.

225 g (8 oz) plain flour
½ level teaspoon mixed spices
½ level teaspoon bicarbonate of soda
175 g (6 oz) light soft brown sugar
100 g (4 oz) butter or margarine
2 eggs, beaten (size 2 or 3)
225 g (8 oz) raisins

50 g (2 oz) currants
50 g (2 oz) currants
50 g (2 oz) cut mixed peel
grated rind of 1 orange
225 g (8 oz) cooking apples, peeled,
    cored and coarsely grated

Preparation time: 25 minutes
Cooking time: 1¼–1½ hours
Heat the oven to 180°C/350°F/Gas Mark 4.

Line a 20 cm (8 inch) round cake tin with greased greaseproof paper. Sift the flour, spice and soda together. Cream the sugar and fat together until very light and fluffy and then gradually beat in the eggs, following each with a spoonful of flour. Fold the remaining flour followed by the dried fruits, peel, orange rind and apples. Mix well, turn into the prepared tin and level the top. Cook in a moderate oven for 1¼–1½ hours until firm to the touch. Cool for a few minutes in the tin before turning out. Leave until cold, then store in an airtight container for 24 hours before eating.

Freezing recommended: for up to 2 months.

Cranberry Teabread

This is my favourite teabread. It is equally good served in thin slices or thick wedges and can be spread lightly with butter or served plain.

225 g (8 oz) plain flour
1½ level teaspoon baking powder
½ level teaspoon bicarbonate of soda
50 g (2 oz) butter or margarine
175 g (6 oz) light soft brown sugar
grated rind of 1 orange

75 g (3 oz) shelled walnuts or pecans,
    chopped
50 g (2 oz) sultanas
100 g (4 oz) cranberries, roughly
    chopped (fresh or frozen)
4 tablespoons orange juice
1 egg (size 2), beaten

Preparation time: *20 minutes*
Cooking time: *1¼ hours*
Heat the oven to 180°C/350°F/Gas Mark 4.

Grease and line a loaf tin approx. 23 x 12.5 x 7.5 cm (9 x 5 x 3 inches) with greased greaseproof or non–stick baking paper. Sift the flour, baking powder and bicarbonate of soda into a bowl. Add the fat and rub in until the mixture resembles fine breadcrumbs. Stir in the sugar, orange rind, nuts and raisins. Mix the cranberries, orange juice and the egg together and add to the rest of the ingredients. Mix lightly just to blend then turn into the pre-pared tin. Bake in a moderate oven for about 1¼ hours until firm to the touch, well risen and golden brown. Turn out on to a wire rack and leave to cool. Wrap in foil until required. It will keep for at least a week in a cool place.

Freezing recommended: *for up to 3 months*

Victoria Sandwich

This is the basic cake and can be flavoured in a great variety of ways.

150 g (6 oz) butter or margarine　　*150 g (6 oz) self–raising flour, sifted*
150 g (6 oz) caster sugar　　　　　*few drops of vanilla esence*
3 eggs (size 1 or 2)　　　　　　　 *1 tablespoon cold water*

Preparation time: *20 minutes*
Cooking time: *25 minutes*
Heat the oven to 190°C/375°F/Gas Mark 5.

Grease two 20 cm (8 inch) round sandwich tins and line the bases with greased greaseproof or non–stick baking paper; or dredge with flour. Cream the fat and the sugar together until light and fluffy and very pale in colour. Beat in the eggs, one at a time, following each with a spoonful of flour. Fold the remaining flour into the mixture with the essence and water. Divide between the tins, level the tops and bake in a moderately hot oven for about 20–25 minutes or until well risen and firm to the touch. Cool in the tin for about a minute, then turn out onto wire racks and leave to cool. Sandwich together with jam and sprinkle the top with caster or sifted icing sugar.

Variations:
Chocolate – replace 25 g (1 oz) of the flour with sifted cocoa powder and add ½ level teaspoon baking powder.
Coffee – omit the vanilla essence and replace the water with coffee essence or 1½ level tablespoons instant coffee dissolved in 1 tablespoon boiling water and cooled.
Orange or lemon – omit the vanilla essence and add the finely grated rind of 1 orange or lemon and replace the water with fruit juice.

Freezing recommended, *unfilled: for up to 4 months*

Bara Brith

Although more often made with a yeast dough this Welsh speciality currant bread produces a delicious teabread without the yeast. Bara means 'bread' in Welsh, whilst 'brith' is speckled and hence the description of currant bread.

225 g (8 oz) self–raising flour
pinch of salt
1 level teaspoon mixed spice
50 g (2 oz) butter or nargarine
50 g (2 oz) caster sugar
grated rind of 1 lemon

100 g (4 oz) currants
75 g (3 oz) black treacle
1 egg (size 2 or 3), beaten
½ level teaspoon bicarbonate of soda
100 ml (4 fl oz) milk

Preparation time: *20 minutes*
Cooking time: *1¼ hours*
Heat the oven to 180°C/350°F/Gas Mark 4.

Grease and line a 900 g (2 lb) loaf tin. Sift the flour, salt and spice into a bowl and rub in the fat until the mixture resembles fine breadcrumbs, then stir in the sugar, lemon rind and currants and mix well. Add the treacle, egg and bicarbonate of soda dissolved in the milk and beat until evenly mixed and smooth. Turn into the prepared tin and bake in a moderate oven for about 1¼ hours or until firm to the touch. Turn out and cool on a wire rack then wrap in foil for at least 24 hours before serving. Serve sliced and buttered.

Freezing recommended: *for up to 2 months*

Gingerbread

A moist gingery cake made by the melting method, which improves with keeping if it hasn't been eaten too quickly.

225 g (8 oz) plain flour
1 level teaspoon mixed spice
2 level teaspoons ground ginger
1 level teaspoon bicarbonate of soda
100 g (4 oz) butter or margarine

50 g (2 oz) dark soft brown sugar
50 g (2 oz) black treacle or molasses
150 g (6 oz) golden syrup
2 eggs (size 2 or 3), beaten
150 ml (¼ pint) milk or soured milk

Preparation time: *20 minutes*
Cooking time: *1¼–1½ hours*
Heat the oven to 150°C/300°F/Gas Mark 2.

Grease and line an 18 cm (7 inch) deep square cake tin with greased grease-proof or non–stick baking paper. Sift the flour, spice, ginger and soda together in a bowl. Put in the butter, sugar, treacle and syrup into a saucepan and heat gently until melted; alternatively melt in the microwave oven. Take care not to overheat or let it reach anywhere near boiling point; then cool until lukewarm. Add the melted mixture, eggs and milk to the dry ingredients and beat well until smooth and bubbly. Pour into the prepared tin and bake in a cool oven for 1¼–1½ hours or until firm to the touch and a skewer inserted in the centre comes out clean. Cool in the tin and then turn out onto a wire rack.

Store in an airtight container for up to 2 months. As gingerbreads improve with keeping it is a good idea to make this one 2–3 days at least before required.

PARTY FOODS
INTRODUCTION

Parties come in all shapes and forms and at most a certain amount of food is served. The ones with simple nibbles, dips, bowls of crisps, French bread, cheese and pâté, are easy, but when the party becomes a little more elaborate and the numbers increase, the poor cook sometimes has quite a task. The recipes given here provide ideas for parties of up to 20 (which is quite easily doubled) for serving either a hot meal with salads, which really requires a seat and a knife and fork to do it justice, or a cold buffet which can be eaten 'on the hoof' with simply a plate and a fork.

The most important thing to remember about a party is to be organized. Do not be tempted to leave the shopping, the flowers or the cooking to the very last minute because something is bound to crop up and consequently seriously delay your plans. Organize the drinks in advance, order from a reputable wine merchant you know of who will more than likely lend you the glasses you require; shop in advance, cook in advance – some dishes can be frozen – arrange your flowers and set what tables are needed. Leave only the essentials to do at the last minute. In this way you should have ample time to get youself ready, serve the meal to your guests without getting in a flap and enjoy the party just as much as everyone else.

HOT MENU FOR TWENTY

Avocado and Crab Cocktails

or

Soused Pink Trout Fillets

Duck With Orange And Cranberry Sauce

Brown Rice and Peanut Salad
Red Cabbage and Leek Medley
Mixed Salad with Fennel and Watercress

Chocolate Blackcurrant Gâteau
Peach and Banana Syllabubs

Avocado and Crab Cocktails

Serves 12

6 ripe avocados
lemon juice
3 x 75 g (3 oz) cartons chilled crab pâté
4 level tablespoons soured cream or
thick set natural yogurt

finely grated rind of ½ lemon
salt and pepper
lettuce leaves or watercress
12 lemon slices to garnish

Preparation time: 25 minutes

Halve the avocados, remove the stones and peel each carefully. Cut each
half into 5 or 6 slices and immerse in lemon juice. Combine the crab pâté,
soured cream or yogurt and lemon rind andadd the seasonings to taste. *To
assemble:* arrange small lettuce leaves or watercress on 12 small plates. Drain
the avocados and arrange 5 or 6 slices in a fan shape on each plate. Spoon
crab pâté over one end of the avocados and garnish with a lemon twist.
Cover with cling–film. Do not assemble more than an hour before serving
or the avocado may discolour. Serve with melba toast and butter.

Soused Pink Trout Fillets

Serves 12

6 pink trout fillets (approx 675 g/1½ lb)
    or 12 small pink trout fillets
300 ml (½ pint) water
4 tablespoons white wine vinegar
4 tablespoons lemon juice
1 onion, peeled and very thinly sliced

1 level teaspoon whole black pepper-
    corns
1 level teaspoon caster sugar
3–4 bay leaves (preferably fresh)
chopped parsley to garnish

Preparation time: 20 minutes
Cooking time: 15 minutes
Heat the oven to 150°C/300°F/Gas Mark 2.

Cut each fillet of trout in half if large, into equal sized portions and lay in a
shallow dish, close together but not overlapping. Place the water, vinegar,
lemon juice, onion,peppercorns and sugar in a saucepan and bring to the
boil then simmer for 5 minutes. Lay the bay leaves over the fish, then pour
the marinade over. Cover and cook in a cool oven for 15 minutes. Remove
and cool; then chill thoroughly. Serve on small plates, almost drained, but
with pieces of onion on top. Sprinkle with parsley and serve with French
bread and butter.

Duck with Orange and Cranberry Sauce

Duck portions are available both fresh and frozen from the supermarkets in wing and leg portions, and boneless breasts.

Serves 20

20 duck portions
salt and pepper
900 ml (1½ pint) good stock
150 ml (¼ pint) red wine or port
150 ml (¼ pint) orange juice (not squash)
3 tablespoons lemon juice

1 level tablespoon tomato purée
1 teaspoon Worcestershire sauce
3 level tablespoons flour
grated rind of 3 oranges
2 x 185 g (6½ oz) jars cranberry sauce
orange wedges and watercress to garnish

Preparation time: 45 minutes
Cooking time: 1 hour
Heat the oven to 200°C/400°F/Gas Mark 6.

Trim the duck portions of any excess fat, then prick the skins all over with a fork and place in two roasting tins in a single layer. Sprinkle lightly with salt and pepper, if liked, and cook in a fairly hot oven for 45–50 minutes, basting once during cooking, until well browned and crisp and cooked through. Meanwhile combine the stock, wine, orange and lemon juices, tomato purée and Worcestershire sauce. Remove the duck and keep warm. Pour off all the fat, just leaving the pan juices. Stir the flour into these and cook for a minute or so until beginning to colour, then gradually add the stock mixture and bring to the boil. Simmer for 3–4 minutes, stirring occasionally. Strain into a saucepan and add the orange rind and cranberry sauce and simmer for 5 minutes. Adjust the seasonings and replace the duck in roasting tins or casseroles and pour the sauce over. Keep warm until required. Serve garnished with orange wedges and watercress.

Note: if cooked the day before, re-cook in a moderate oven for about 40 minutes. If frozen, thaw completely then re-cook in the same way.

Brown Rice and Peanut Salad

550 g (1¼ lb) American style brown rice
salt
100 g (4 oz) dry roasted peanuts

½ head celery, trimmed and thinly sliced
1–2 green peppers, deseeded, sliced and blanched

Preparation time: 20 minutes
Cooking time: 30 minutes

Cook the rice in plenty of boiling water until just tender – about 25 minutes; or following the directions on the packet. Drain, rinse under cold water and drain again. Turn into a bowl. Add the peanuts, celery and well drained peppers, mix well and turn into a serving bowl. Cover with cling–film and chill until required.

Alternatively this salad may be served hot – put into greased ovenproof dishes and cover with foil; heat in a moderate oven (180°C/350°F/Gas Mark 4) for about 30 minutes; or cover with cling–film and heat in a microwave oven set on High/100% and cook for 3 minutes, stir well and heat for a further 2 minutes.

Red Cabbage and Leek Medley

1 red cabbage (about 900 g (2 lb)
1 large or 2 small leeks, trimmed

3 green–skinned eating apples
lemon juice

Preparation time: 20 minutes

Trim the cabbage, quarter and remove the cores and then shred finely. Slice the leeks very thinly, washing those parts which look dirty and then drain and dry thoroughly. Mix the cabbage and leeks together thoroughly and store in a polythene bag in the refrigerator until ready to serve. Core and chop or slice the apples and dip in lemon juice. Add to the salad, turn into a bowl and serve with French dressing (see page 44).

Mixed Salad with Fennel and Watercress

2 heads fennel
1 bunch radishes, trimmed
½–1 head Chinese leaves

2 carrots, peeled and cut into narrow
    sticks
2 bunches watercress, trimmed

Preparation time: 20 minutes

Remove the feathery part of the fennel and use for garnish. Trim the remainder, chop and put into a bowl. Slice the radishes thinly, slice the Chinese leaves and add to the fennel with the carrots and watercress. Mix well, turn into a serving bowl, cover with cling–film and chill until required. Serve with French dressing (see page 44).

Chocolate Blackcurrant Gâteau

Serves 12

175 g (6 oz) butter or margarine
175 g (6 oz) caster or light soft brown
    sugar

3 eggs (size 2 or 3)
150 g (5 oz) self–raising flour
25 g (1 oz) cocoa

½ level teaspoon baking powder
few drops vanilla essence
1 tablespoon cold water

Filling:
450 g (1 lb) blackcurrants

4 tablespoons water
approx 100 g (4 oz) caster sugar
1 level tablespoon arrowroot
300 ml (½ pint) double cream
3 tablespoons rum or brandy (optional)
2–3 kiwi fruit

Preparation time: *1 hour*
Cooking time: *40 minutes*
Heat the oven to 190°C/350°F/Gas Mark 5.

Cream the fat and sugar until very light and fluffy. Beat in the eggs, one at a time, following each with a spoonful of flour. Sift the remaining flour with the cocoa and baking powder and fold into the mixture followed by the essence and water. Divide between the three 20 cm (8 inch) greased and base–lined round sandwich tins and bake in a moderately hot oven for 15–20 minutes until well risen and firm to the touch. Turn out onto wire racks and leave until cold.

Meanwhile stew the blackcurrants in the water until tender, add the sugar to taste and heat until dissolved. Blend the arrowroot with the minimum of cold water, add to the fruit and bring to the boil, stirring until thickened. Turn into a bowl, cover and leave until cold.

To assemble: whip the cream until stiff. Place one cake on a serving dish and sprinkle with 1 tablespoon rum. Spread with a quarter of the cream and just over ⅓ of the blackcurrant filling. Cover with the second cake and repeat. Cover with the last layer and sprinkle with remaining rum. Put the remaining cream into a piping bag fitted with a large star vegetable nozzle and pipe a continuous twisted circle of cream on top of the gâteau about 2.5 cm (1 inch) in from the edge. Spoon the remaining blackcurrant filling into the centre of the cream ring. Peel and slice the kiwi fruit and arrange whole slices around the top outside edge of the gâteau and halved slices standing up between the cream and blackcurrant topping. Chill for at least 2 hours.

Peach and Banana Syllabubs

Serves 12

4 bananas
2 tablespoons lemon juice
3–4 peaches or nectarines
3 tablespoons rum or brandy

Syllabub:
700 ml (1¼ pints) double cream

10 tablespoons dry white wine
2 tablespoons lemon juice
4 level tablespoons caster sugar
finely grated rind of ½ lemon
finely grated rind of 1 orange
coarsely grated orange rind for
    decoration

Preparation time: *25 minutes*

Peel the bananas, slice and put into a bowl with the lemon juice; toss well. Slice the peaches into another bowl, add the rum and toss well. Put the cream, wine, lemon juice and sugar into a bowl and whisk until stiff. Fold in the fruit rinds and put into a piping bag fitted with a large star nozzle. Drain the bananas and mix with the peaches and rum. Divide between 12 glasses and pipe the syllabub over each one ending in a peak on top. Sprinkle with coarsely grated orange rind and chill until required. They can be prepared up to 4 hours in advance.

COLD FORK BUFFET

Pissaladière

Salmagundy

Rare Roast Beef with Mustard Mayonnaise

Stuffed Pasta Shells

Stuffed Tomatoes

Nectarine Salad

Ruby Wine Cup

Pissaladière

Sometimes this is made from a bread base, sometimes from pastry; here I've used a packet of instant bread mix to speed up the process.

Serves 10–20

1 packet bread mix (brown or white)

Topping:
350 g (12 oz) onion, peeled and thinly sliced
2 cloves garlic, crushed
2 tablespoons oil
675 g (1½ lb) tomatoes, peeled and sliced

2 level tablespoons tomato purée
175 g (6 oz) mushrooms, trimmed and sliced
salt and pepper
1½–2 level teaspoons dried oregano
1 can anchovy fillets, drained
½ green pepper, cut into narrow strips and blanched
black olives

Preparation time: *30 minutes, plus rising time*
Cooking time: *45 minutes*
Heat the oven to 220°C/425°F/Gas Mark 7.

Make up the bread mix following the directions on the packet. For the topping, fry the onions and garlic in the oil for about 15–20 minutes until soft; then add the tomatoes and tomato purée and cook gently for about 10 minutes. Add the mushrooms, seasonings and oregano and continue to cook until the mixture is thick. Cool. Roll out the bread dough and use to line a greased roasting tin approx 30 x 25 cm (12 x 10 inches) taking the dough about 2.5 cm(1 inch) up the sides. Spread the tomato mixture over the dough then garnish with halved strips of anchovy and strips of pepper. Put to rise for about 20–30 minutes or until puffy. Cook in a hot oven for about 35–45 minutes until the dough is lightly browned and feels cooked. Add halved olives to complete the garnish and serve hot or cold, cut into strips or squares.

Freezing recommended: *for up to 6 weeks*

Salmagundy

This is an old–fashioned English dish which always incorporates meat and vegetables, and often game or poultry and fish. It is served as a large mixed platter that is ideal for a fork meal. It can easily be doubled up to serve more people.

Serves 10

675 g (1½ lb) potatoes, peeled boiled and diced
225 g (8 oz) frozen peas, lightly cooked
450 g (1 lb) carrots, peeled, cut into sticks and lightly cooked
150 ml (¼ pint) French dressing (see page 44)
1 clove garlic, crushed
450 g (1 lb) cooked chicken meat, cut into strips

450 g (1 lb) cooked duck, beef or lamb, or a mixture of meats, cut into strips
1 cucumber, sliced
½ head of celery, sliced
225–450 g (½–1 lb) cherry tomatoes
4 hard–boiled eggs, quartered or sliced

To garnish:
parsley sprigs or watercress or frisée
black olives
few whole or peeled prawns (optional)

Preparation time: *30–60 minutes*

The joy of this dish is that it can be put together very quickly or you can spend quite some time arranging the ingredients decoratively in symmetrical designs. Lightly mix the potatoes and peas with about half the carrots and arrange over the base of a large oval platter. Sprinkle with a little dressing to which the garlic has been added. Then layer up the other ingredients either separately or together to make an interesting mixture on the platter, sprinkling lightly with dressing as you go. The idea is that each person takes a spoonful of salmgundy and gets a little of everything. Garnish attractively with carrots, parsley, watercress or frisée, olives and a few prawns, if liked. Chill until required.

Rare Beef Rolls with Mustard Mayonnaise

Makes 20–25

450–675 g (1–1½) piece of fillet steak
salt and pepper
2 cloves garlic, crushed
oil or dripping
150 ml (¼ pint) thick mayonnaise

grated rind of ½ lemon or lime
1 level tablespoon coarse grain mustard
225 g (8 oz) carrots, peeled and cut into narrow strips
cocktail sticks
parsley to garnish

Preparation time: *50 minutes, plus cooling time*
Cooking time: *12–35 minutes*
Heat the oven to 220°C/425°F/Gas Mark 7.

Season the meat, rub well with garlic and pour about 2 tablespoons of oil or dripping over it. Roast in a hot oven allowing about 12 minutes for a 450 g (1 lb) piece for rare or 20 minutes if you like it medium. For a 675 g (1½ lb) piece allow 18 minutes for rare or 30–35 minutes for medium. Remove from the oven, cool and then chill. *To assemble:* combine the mayonnaise with the lemon or lime rind and mustard. The carrots can be used raw; or if preferred, blanch them for 3 minutes, drain and cool. Slice the beef very thinly, spread each piece with a little mustard mayonnaise and put several sticks of carrots on it. Roll up, push on a cocktail stick and put on a platter. Garnish each roll with a sprig of parsley.

Stuffed Pasta Shells

These can be eaten in the fingers if preferred, although it is easier with a fork.

Makes 20

20 large pasta shells
450 g (1 lb) frozen spinach
1–2 cloves garlic, crushed
100 g (4 oz) mature Edam cheese, grated
6 tablespoons soured cream or thick–set natural yogurt
salt and pepper

100 g (4 oz) streaky bacon, crisply fried and crumbled
40 g (1½ oz) toasted hazelnuts, finely chopped
pinch of ground nutmeg
2–3 tablespoons French dressing, (see page 44)

Preparation time: *40 minutes*

Cook the pasta shells in a large saucepan of boiling water for 8–10 minutes or until just tender, then drain thoroughly. Cook the spinach in a saucepan for 10–15 minutes until thoroughly thawed and cooked, then drain and chop finely. Divide the mixture in half. To one half add the garlic, cheese and 3 tablespoons soured cream and season to taste; to the other add the rest of the soured cream, bacon, hazelnuts, seasonings and a pinch of ground nutmeg. Fill the shells with the two mixtures and stand them on a serving dish. Drizzle a little French dressing over each one.

Stuffed Tomatoes

You need fairly small tomatoes for this recipe, where you get about 12 per 450 g (1 lb).

Makes 20

20 small tomatoes
40 g (1½ oz) long grain rice, freshly
  boiled
1 onion, peeled and finely chopped
1 tablespoon oil
1 teaspoon Worcestershire sauce

1 level tablespoon freshly chopped
  parsley
1 hard–boiled egg, coarsely grated
75 g (3 oz) smoked salmon or smoked
  mackerel, chopped
salt and pepper
20 black olives

Preparation time: *30 minutes*

Cut the tops off the tomatoes and scoop out the seeds. Put the rice into a bowl. Fry the onion in the oil until lightly browned, then add to the rice with the Worcestershire sauce and parsley. When cold, add the egg, fish and seasonings to taste. Spoon into the tomatoes, and top each with a black olive. Stand on a platter surrounded by frisée leaves.

Nectarine Salad

A refreshing salad which can also be made using peaches, when available.

Serves 16–20

12 nectarines
6 oranges
grated rind of 1 orange
175 g (6 oz) caster sugar
300 ml (½ pint) water

2–3 tablespoons lemon juice
2–4 tablespoons orange liqueur
  (optional)
6 firm kiwi fruit

Preparation time: *30 minutes*

Halve the nectarines, remove the stones and slice thickly into a shallow bowl. Pare the rind from 1 orange, free of white pith, cut into julienne strips and cook in boiling water for 5 minutes, until tender, then drain. Add the grated orange rind and the juice of all the oranges to the nectarines. Dissolve the sugar in the water, bring to the boil and simmer for 3–4 minutes; remove from the heat, leave to cool and add the lemon juice, and liqueur, if used. Peel and slice the kiwi fruit and mix with the nectarines, pour the syrup overall and mix lightly. Sprinkle with the orange rind, cover and chill before serving.

Ruby Wine Cup

Makes 20 glasses

thinly pared rind of one orange
600 ml (1 pint) water
100 g (4 oz) caster sugar
1 level teaspoon mixed spice

2 cinnamon sticks
3 bottles red wine
150 ml (¼ pint) gin (optional)
2 oranges, thinly sliced

Preparation time: *20 minutes*

Put the strips of orange rind into a saucepan with the water, sugar, spice and cinnamon sticks and heat until the sugar dissolves, then simmer gently for 5 minutes until the rind is tender. Add the wine and bring very slowly to just below boiling point. Just before serving, stir in the gin and float the orange slices on the surface. Reheat gently.

THIRST QUENCHERS

Ginger Special

A refreshing non–alcoholic drink of apple juice and ginger ale flavoured with mint.

Makes 6 glasses (approx 1¼ litres/2¼ pints)

approx 75 ml (1¼ pints) apple juice,
*   chilled*
1 split American ginger ale, chilled

1 split dry ginger ale, chilled
few sprigs of mint
ice cubes

Preparation time: *10 minutes*

Combine the apple juice, ginger ales, mint sprigs and ice cubes in a jug and mix very well. Pour into long glasses, making sure each one has a sprig of mint and drink through straws.

Rosy Wine Cup

A rosé wine, whether still or slightly sparkling, makes a most refreshing and delicious wine cup, ideal to serve at lunch time.

Makes 12–16 glasses (approx 2¼ litres/4 pints)

2 bottles rosé wine, chilled
6–8 tablespoons brandy
2 oranges, thinly sliced
2 lemons, thinly sliced
225 g (8 oz) black grapes, halved and
    depipped

1–2 dessert apples, peeled, cored and
    sliced
900 ml (1½ pints) fizzy lemonade
little crushed ice

Preparation time: 20 minutes

Pour the wine and brandy into a bowl or jug, add the fruit and chill for at least an hour. Just before serving add the lemonade and crushed ice, stir well and serve.

Barbary Ale

Reminiscent of the Barbary Coast with its spices and sunshine, this punch is an excellent thirst quencher.

Makes about 12 glasses (2¼ litres/4 pints)

juice of 4 oranges
thinly pared rind and juice of 1 large
    lemon
600 ml (1 pint) water

50–73 g (2–3 oz) caster sugar
½ level teaspoon ground cinnamon
½ level teaspoon mixed spice
2 litres (3½ pints) ginger beer, chilled

Preparation time: 15 minutes, plus standing time

Put the orange juice, lemon rind and juice, water, sugar and spices into a bowl, mix well and leave to stand for 3–4 hours. Just before serving, strain into a bowl and add the chilled ginger beer. A few slices of lemon may be floated on the top.

Chairman's Special

This cider cup was created by Bertram Bulmer of Bulmer's Cider and is a most delicious drink. He insists that only the very finely pared rind of the lemon is used or the flavour will be spoilt. Use a potato peeler to pare it really thinly, free of all white pith.

Makes up to 20 glasses (approx 3 litres/5½ pints)

Very thinly pared rind of two lemons
175 ml (6 fl oz) medium sherry
2 bottles dry Pomagne, chilled
2 bottles dry white wine, chilled

175 ml (6 fl oz) brandy
175 g (6 oz) raspberries
2 bananas

Preparation time: 20 minutes, plus standing time

Place the lemon rind in a large jug or bowl with the sherry and leave to stand for about 30 minutes. Add the Pomagne, wine and brandy with the raspberries and thinly sliced bananas. Stir well and serve in glasses. Ice cubes or crushed ice may also be added.

Sangria

A favourite Spanish drink which will bring back many happy holiday memories.

Makes 8 glasses (approx 1½ litres/2½ pints)

1 bottle Spanish red wine, chilled
600 ml (1 pint) fizzy lemonade, chilled
2–4 tablespoons brandy (optional)
1 lemon, thinly sliced

1 orange, thinly sliced
few slices apple
ice cubes

Preparation time: 15 minutes

Put all the ingredients into a jug, mix well and add a few ice cubes. Serve in tall glasses with straws, if liked.

Orange Cooler

Just a touch of alcohol can be added if you want that extra zing.

Makes 8–10 glasses (approx 1½ litres/2½ pints)

1 can frozen orange concentrate
water
150 ml (¼ pint) pineapple juice
juice of 2 lemons
2–3 tablespoons Cointreau or Grand

Marnier (optional)
600 ml (1 pint) tonic water, chilled
ice cubes
orange slices
cucumber slices

Preparation time: 15 minutes

Thaw the orange juice and make up with cold water as directed on the can. Add the pineapple juice, lemon juice and liqueur (if used); then chill thoroughly. Just before serving add the tonic water, ice cubes and slices of orange and cucumber.

What is the WI?

If you have enjoyed this book, the chances are that you would enjoy belonging to the largest Women's organization in the country – the Women's Institutes.

We are friendly, go-ahead, like minded women, who derive enormous satisfaction from all the movement has to offer. The list is long – you can make new friends, have fun and companionship, visit new places, develop new skills, take part in community services, fight local campaigns, become a WI market producer, and play an active role in an organization which has a national voice.

The WI is the only women's organization in the country which owns an adult education establishment. At Denman College, you can take a course in anything from car maintenance to paper sculpture, from book-binding to yoga, or cordon bleu cookery to fly-fishing.

All you need to do to join is write to us here at the **National Federation of Women's Institutes, 104 New Kings Road, London SW6 4LY,** or telephone 071 371 9300, and we will put you in touch with WIs in your immediate locality. We hope to hear from you.

Home & Country is the official magazine of the NFWI. The first issue was produced in March 1919 and it has been published monthly ever since – even throughout the War! Its aim is to provide a link between members at all levels and, as such, acts as a forum for news and views. There is also a broad range of general features and comment on rural and environmental issues, alongside health, cookery, craft, fashion and beauty, as well as reader holidays, competitions and special offers. For details of subscription and advertising rates, write to *Home & Country*, 104 Kings Road, London SW6 4LY.

Rosemary Wadey has been cookery editor of *Home & Country* since 1969, as well as working as a cookery writer and freelance home economist. Previously she was the head of the Food Advisory Department at the Good Housekeeping Institute. She has had over 25 cookery books published on a wide range of subjects. She is married with two daughters and lives in West Sussex.